RADICAL OUTCOMES

RADICAL OUTCOMES

how to create extraordinary teams
that get tangible results

JULIANA STANCAMPIANO

WILEY

Published by John Wiley & Sons, Inc., Hoboken, New Jersey.
Published simultaneously in Canada.

For general information on our other products and services or for technical support, please contact our Customer Care Department within the United States at (800) 762-2974, outside the United States at (317) 572-3993 or fax (317) 572-4002.

Wiley publishes in a variety of print and electronic formats and by print-on-demand. Some material included with standard print versions of this book may not be included in e-books or in print-on-demand. If this book refers to media such as a CD or DVD that is not included in the version you purchased, you may download this material at http://booksupport.wiley.com. For more information about Wiley products, visit www.wiley.com.

Library of Congress Cataloging-in-Publication Data

Names: Stancampiano, Juliana, 1978- author.
Title: Radical outcomes : how to create extraordinary teams that get tangible
  results / Juliana Stancampiano.
Description: Hoboken : Wiley, 2019. | Includes index. |
Identifiers: LCCN 2018041055 (print) | LCCN 2018043027 (ebook) |
  ISBN 9781119524281 (ePub) | ISBN 9781119524298 (ePDF) |
  ISBN 9781119524250 (hardback)
Subjects: LCSH: Selling. | Teams in the workplace. | Leadership. | BISAC:
  BUSINESS & ECONOMICS / Management. | BUSINESS & ECONOMICS / Leadership. |
  BUSINESS & ECONOMICS / Sales & Selling.
Classification: LCC HF5438.25 (ebook) | LCC HF5438.25 .S723 2019 (print) |
  DDC 658.4/022—dc23
LC record available at https://lccn.loc.gov/2018041055

Cover Design: Wiley
Cover Image: © Oxygen Learning, LLC

Printed in the United States of America

V10006317_112118

For my parents: my mother, who taught me that learning doesn't happen only from a textbook, and my father, who modeled leading a radically productive team, and both of them for challenging the norms, being values driven, and teaching me the importance of doing the work. And to my kids, Alexander and Aylina, for being my biggest fans. I love you all.

Contents

The Why

They always say time changes things, but you actually have to change them yourself.

—Andy Warhol

The conference room door at Omen, Inc., opened with a sudden CLACK, and 10 people in pressed designer shirts, spring dresses, and well-appointed shoes emerged. Some of them checked their phones, others joined new conference calls while standing by the windows in the hallway, and several made their way to the restrooms around the corner.

The open door to the conference room revealed a long, boardroom-style table littered with printouts, notepads, laptops, glasses of water, and soda cans. A screen at the front of the room showed a slide: "BREAK, 15 mins." Several men and women were still inside, standing next to the windows, talking in small groups, or helping themselves to the fruit salad and protein bars at the caterers' table.

Maya Rodriguez, a woman in her mid-forties with dark hair in tight ringlets held back with a silver and turquoise barrette, exited into the hallway, gesturing as she spoke to Garrett Stokes, a man who appeared to be a few years younger, his pressed orange shirt rolled up at the sleeves. Together they walked slowly away from the conference room. Maya checked her phone while talking.

"Yep. Like turning a battleship. We'll kick the project off immediately," she affirmed, scrolling through an email with one hand.

"I can't believe how long it took to get all of them in that room working together," Garrett said, still a little shocked.

"Better late than never," she answered. "Look at where we are after nine months of squinting at metrics and data, and all the research we had to do. I think the recommendation makes sense. It's just the time frame is pretty insane."

She gestured back into the room.

"Think about it, Garrett. When does this company get business managers and GMs from so many different areas in the same room? And VP level. That was all good discussion and I agree – creating the new sales roles is the right move for where the business is headed. It's kind of exciting... finally, we are recognizing something different."

"Sure, but it took us the better part of a year to all agree on a direction. Now we're in a big crunch to get these people ramped." He looked directly at Maya. "Which will be... interesting."

They stopped near a window and surveyed the courtyard. Maya's shoulders dropped in resignation as she exhaled.

"I know. Rivers said flat out – it has to be done differently."

She looked back toward the conference room.

"I think we still have about 10 minutes, right? I'm going to give Jack the heads-up – his office is in this building."

She parted ways with Garrett and walked down the hall, turned a corner, passed an office with an open door – then stopped suddenly and backed up. Walking to the open door, she knocked on the doorjamb and poked her head in without waiting for a reply. "Jack."

Jack's back was toward the door, but as soon as he heard Maya's voice he turned quickly. She continued without small talk.

"I have to go back into the meeting, but the upshot is that it's happening. I gave you the heads-up last quarter. So I hope you've thought about what your team is going to do."

Jack raised his eyebrows. "Well, we've had a lot on our plate –"

Maya interrupted him.

"I get it. Lots of people have lots of plates with lots of stuff on them. Your team needs to be ready to engage. Probably should have happened sooner. We can talk at five when the session is over – I have to get back and chat with Garrett again about how quickly we can get going."

She headed for the door, then paused and turned back.

"Just so you know, the feedback from the room wasn't great. People like your team, Jack, but it just takes too long for the programs to come together, and the sellers aren't ramped fast enough. The business managers aren't happy with the content. They were nice about it – well, mostly nice – well, maybe some of it wasn't nice at all. But what you need to know is, Rivers himself said this program has to be different. You'll need to put your best lead on it."

"Okay, right," Jack smiled. Maya looked closely at him. *Why does it always seem like he's going to show me that car from the back of the lot, instead of the one I want in the showroom?* she wondered. "So how long do we have, Maya?"

"Two months. They plan to have the first new hires in two months. Well, technically, 10 weeks from now. So that's better than two months, right?"

Without waiting for a response, she left the office and walked briskly down the hall.

■ ■ ■

The story that is unfolding here, and will continue to develop throughout this book, is a story about the world of work. It's our world and your world, where directives are initiated, people are engaged to do work, stuff is created. But it's also a world where expectations are built and then not lived up to. Where commitments are made, and yet no one can point to the results. And where random things happen, along with significant wasted time, energy, and money – none of which are trivial resources for any person.

The world of Maya and the executives in her meeting is one where she, her peers, and her superiors all feel as if they are trying to turn a 45,000-ton military vessel 180 degrees. And as she turned to Jack – whose remit, we'll learn, is to help with the steering – we sensed the friction that already existed, a situation in which change needed to happen, fast, but isn't happening much at all. Just what kind of change is afoot will be revealed in the following chapters.

What's really going on?

The World Has Changed, and So Must We

The world has changed. The way we communicate and connect with each other, the way we run our lives – it's all changed. Consumers and buyers today have information at their fingertips, more discerning criteria for how they spend their money, and continuously shifting expectations. Amazon CEO Jeff Bezos describes customers as "divinely discontent,"[1] a positive and nuanced celebration of the vigilance that businesses must have to keep up with customers. To keep up with customers, many business leaders have recognized that just having great products isn't enough. They must also create great experiences for their customers. And they must do it by leveraging the increasingly complex technology landscape that has become part of life. The demand for excellent customer experiences, powered by the innovative technology companies that have created them, has disrupted every business in every industry, forcing all kinds of transformation – and this holds equally true for businesses that don't serve consumers.

Consider the implications of disruption and transformation on all of the different professions, domains of expertise, and standards of practice that exist in an organization. What if that expertise doesn't work any longer, because so much has changed? For large organizations, when it doesn't work, it doesn't work at a massive scale.

For Maya and the executives in this meeting, who have made a big bet to create new sales roles, this is a scary reality. How do they figure out how to manage all the disruption? Who's going to tell them what to do to execute on the decision that took nine months to formulate? We'll learn more about how Maya faces this reality and how the challenge calls into question all familiar approaches. Her peers and mentors are intelligent people who have been successful. But something isn't right, and it's getting worse all the time. It prompts one very important, central, and potentially uncomfortable question: Why do you have a job? How can you be more instrumental in helping your people to succeed?

What Does Insanity Feel Like?

Maya's world probably sounds familiar. We've been there and can relate to what she feels: insanity. She's part of an organization where the leaders feel like they've been doing the same thing over and over and expecting a different result. This feeling of insanity can manifest itself in different ways, depending on the altitude levels of people in the organization.

In our view, we think of the organization in three parts:

1. C-level and executives, who set the direction of the business
2. Leaders of teams who guide people toward the outcomes required for the business
3. Teams who must make those outcomes happen through interactions with customers

Each of these groups has a role to play in ensuring that a business moves forward, can adapt to change, and survive. But a business is more complex than just having three simple groups or altitude levels: there are functions and departments such as Research and Development, Engineering, Sales, Customer Service, Marketing, and Finance. These functions have a simple intention: drive the business forward. But as a business grows, things get complicated in scope and scale. The more customers buy from a business, the larger the enterprise, and the more people are needed in functions. Overlays are created. Some roles within the organization have more frequent interaction with customers than others. Some functions in the organization are there to support other functions.

With this in mind, when we think about what's happening in the workplace, we mainly think about the relationship between an *enabling function* (such as Marketing, Sales or Field Support, Learning and Development, Product Groups, vertical Business Units), the *audience* of customer-facing people that function as supports (such as customer service agents, salespeople, consultants, partner account managers), and how that impacts value to *customers* (whoever your business sells to, be it consumers, other businesses, or partners). And on top of all that is the Executive function, setting strategy and direction for the business. See the definitions in the Glossary of Terms at the end of this chapter, as we will use the terms *Executive, Enablement, Audience,* and *Customer* to mean these specific positions of purpose. Figure 1.1 shows these different groups of people and the altitude levels in an organization.

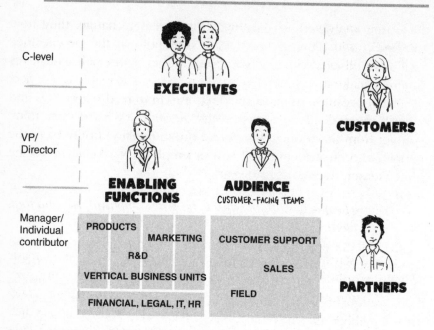

F<small>IGURE</small> 1.1   Organizational Groups and Altitude Levels

We believe that every person in the workplace is in one of these four categories. Even if your job is in Finance, or Human Resources, or IT, we are quite sure that if you ask yourself the question above – *why do I have a job?* – for those specific departments, you are there as part of an enabling function.

At the same time, it's worth pointing out that over the past decade, the word "Enablement" has made its way into functions and job titles, particularly as it relates to selling. The term "Sales Enablement"[2] is now associated with an entire industry of technology, consulting, conferences and practitioners, and is a profession in its own right.

Regardless of where you sit in your function – Executive, Enablement, or Audience – you probably feel the insanity. Here is what that looks like.

CEOs and Executives Feel Like Their Investments Are Going into a Black Hole

Maya, her colleague Garrett, and the general managers and vice presidents who were in that conference room, are all of the same mind: things have come to a head. After gathering information, doing the analysis, and creating a directive for change, they now need help with that shift, but have little faith in the people they routinely call on to help. And the issue isn't personal: executives routinely make investments, but then it seems impossible to connect the dots to results. In interviews that we conducted with CEOs and other business leaders, we asked the question, "What do you think you get from the money you spend on your sales support? On the people who create learning for your employees?" We received the same answer, over and over again:

We have people who create stuff to keep us compliant. Beyond that, it's not clear.

This is startling. But not unrecognizable. The investments made to help people adapt to disruptive change – such as retooling sales forces, changing product portfolios, rethinking go-to-market strategies, and going through structural re-orgs – aren't moving the needle.[3]

Why would a business leader make investments that don't have a result? We answer that question in Chapter 4, "Let Go of What You Know," when we talk about the habits we hold onto, even when they don't work.

ENABLEMENT TEAMS FEEL UNDERSTAFFED

Several clicks down below the C-suite are the people who do lots of different kinds of work. Here is where the rubber meets the road. And there is friction and frustration here as well. Enablement teams can't keep up with all of the stuff that the business says they need to accomplish. The demands never end and the results are never good enough.

While there are different areas that people are responsible for, the common theme is one of frenetic activity and an inability to keep pace with what feels like a moving target of requirements. We've heard a range of frustration from different types of managers in the middle of their organizations, struggling to keep morale high, stay well-staffed, and show productivity.

 ◆ **Manager of Enablement:** I'm frustrated at our pace of design and delivery, and I'm under the gun to justify our impact on the business. How can we be faster and more relevant?

- ◆ **Developers and Designers:** It never stops – all the different requests. I have no idea how to keep up or prioritize. It's so hard to know what's really needed for people to be successful!
- ◆ **Subject Matter Expert:** I love what I do, but no one seems to understand it when I tell them about it. I'm caught in between trying to just do my job, and then being asked to teach other people – it's like doing two different jobs.
- ◆ **Trainer:** I can't just show my audiences yet another PowerPoint that I have to change to make relevant. Why can't the training designers give me something more engaging?

THE AUDIENCE IS OVERWHELMED WITH THE NOISE AND LACK OF RELEVANCE

Pick up 10 annual reports for a publicly traded company or listen to 10 earnings calls. How many of them contain statements from the CEO speaking to the importance of their sales force or their customer-facing employees? Service agents, sellers, delivery personnel, baristas, flight attendants – anyone in a business who has regular interaction with a customer or a partner – has a different view than a noncustomer facing employee and is susceptible to the customer's "divine discontent" if they aren't properly prepared to engage. In our view, this group – the Audience, as we defined it earlier – is so critical in a business and yet, is astonishingly underserved. As we explore in this chapter, the people who need the most guidance on how to be successful are unfortunately flooded with so much information, there is no possible way for them to absorb it, let alone change what they know and do to help a business adapt.

There you have it: three levels of insanity, manifested in random stuff that doesn't move the needle. What's the implication?

There's Only So Much That People Can Learn at One Time

Everything we are writing about has to do with adapting our incredibly complex organizations, processes, and systems to how the world has changed. There are new technologies to navigate, new processes to engineer and adopt, and entirely new conversations that need to take place at work and with customers.

There is so much pressure to change, and seemingly so little time to do it. Under pressure, decision makers make investments that appear to assume we live in a science fiction film, where knowledge and skills can be magically uploaded *en masse.* An almost mystical belief prevails, where all you need to do is send those salespeople, managers, or engineers to a five-day training course, and all of the company's problems will be solved.

Of course, most people don't believe a five-day course will magically transform their teams. There are other things that will take place that will help those people, right? But who is thinking about what those things are? Who is deciding how much content is too much? And who is factoring in that learning a concept, skill, or piece of knowledge happens over time, not at the moment of introduction, and not even the fifth time or ninth time that a new process has been introduced? Who is thinking about the audience, and then the customer or other person the audience has to interact with?

Why is it so hard to meet someone where they're at, and help them from there?

We often encounter people who hold on to the belief that the way to help educate, inform, or equip someone for success is to make sure that all of the content is given to the person *all at once.* There is *little to no thought* applied to spacing out the material. Executives and managers spend what they think is a reasonable amount of money, time, or both. The enablement teams create stuff based on all of the content they want to get across, and then believe they've achieved their objective simply by tallying up its consumption. But in the end, the sheer volume of information that is unleashed to the audience just feels like a firehose of information and, instead of being retained, evaporates quickly.

There are studies that show how information overload, multitasking, and prolonged repetition actually impair productivity, performance, and decision making.[4] Yet, year after year, billions of dollars are spent on initiatives, programs, change efforts, revamps, classes, new technologies, and courseware. What's the result? A major increase in noise.

Herein lies the reason that Maya had to share feedback with Jack that wasn't so great.

How Do People Learn New Things?

The process of learning is a refinement of what we already know, to increase the degree of sophistication in applying new information to new scenarios and situations. The conversations that we engage in today are the result of a learning process that started as a baby's babbling. A child learns the simplest version of running a complicated pattern downfield by just toddling forward. Even the most gifted, intuitive, athlete in a given sport first learned the basics of what will become a complex, improvisational running pattern downfield – from just wobbling forward between Mommy and Daddy.

That's what learning is: taking that which we already know how to do and adding a bit of new stuff to it. Every old memory is changed when it is recalled to mind. Every time we consider something new, the old thought is stored with its new processing. This process is called *reconsolidation*. Our most impressionable times occur early in life, from birth through our early twenties. We all create a mental map of experiences, reactions, and cues that we store away. These are the building blocks for how we are going to synthesize information as an adult.

When it comes to learning something new, the majority of existing methods tend to put the onus on the individual to integrate that new content or skill into their own model. In the case of learning at work – where we pick up Maya's story – content is most often shoved at people in great quantities with random objectives, and then somehow, people are expected to assimilate it immediately into productive action . . . like magic.

But people don't actually change that quickly. It happens over time. We have to *want* to change, and before committing, we need to see how change can benefit us. Then we might slowly change over time, to the point that when we realize we have changed, it's normally a year later. When we look back, we can begin to quantify the changes.

Science tells us that the learning process is not magical. It's actually well known that the best forms of learning build from the outside in, creating the basic crude understanding and then building upon this with increasing sophistication, through experiential and iterative means.

An analogy to consider would be a stack of books. The stack represents our knowledge and skills at any given time, with each book loosely representing a domain area. The knowledge and skills are represented cohesively on many separate pages.

When we learn new things, we are constantly undergoing reconsolidation in the brain. In effect, we are adding new pages to books – actually, taking books out of the stack, opening them up, reacquainting ourselves with them, inserting pages in different places in each book, and returning them to the shelf where we have now built the overall stack.[5]

The way any learning audience is engaged today, it is as if someone is trying to pile one big new book onto the top of the stack and expecting that it will have an impact. The student is supposed to get it, apply it, and somehow start behaving "better." But in reality, that big new book just falls off the stack, its pages scattered, with only a smattering of its information staying with the stack. At best, we might be able to recall having seen the cover somewhere at some point.

Information overload tends to manifest itself in the following ways:

The amount of content that people are expected to process and digest, let alone change their behavior, is overwhelming. We did a process audit with one client and found that new-hire salespeople would routinely receive 50 emails announcing all of the "mandatory" training they were expected to complete. The result? 100% of the salespeople opted out of 100% of the training.

Content is deployed regardless of its cognitive ease. We conducted hundreds of content audits where 100% of the information that was deemed necessary to know was delivered in homogenous bulleted text, PowerPoint decks with over 50 slides, or slides with voice-over explanations. What recipient would declare themselves "trained" after this?

Content is not connected to a plausible, measurable goal. In our reviews of thousands of courses, modules, online learning classes, and instructor-led materials, only a handful of the content could be connected to a specific, measurable outcome.

If this is the case, *where* and *when* is learning actually happening? It's in that seemingly magical process, happening on the job, in front of customers, with peers and managers, during free time, online, and in whatever interests a person may have. Or, at worst, learning is not happening at all. Ask a salesperson whether they felt the formal training they received was valuable and helped with their success, and see what they say.

Relying on Magic Is Costing Crazy Amounts of Money

The uncomfortable conclusion that can be drawn from this is: decision makers are wasting their company's money. At best, they are investing in something and have no idea what the return actually is, so they write it off as the cost of doing business. And this is a lot of money – the L&D industry represents a market of $140B spent on technology, tools, and content.[6]

Could it be that Enablement teams – the people in charge of creating materials for their audiences – are not truly understanding the business outcome that they are working to fix?

No wonder Maya and her colleagues are frustrated.

Of course, there are studies showing a general correlation between learning opportunities and success of the company. We believe that general correlation isn't good enough when a company's investment – and the success of its people – is at stake. Even when something is measured, these types of metrics tend to be impossible to correlate to results. There are countless ways to conduct assessments and knowledge checks, or to survey employees to ask what they think. Do these measurements connect to whether someone achieves their quota? Or whether a customer is delighted with an interaction?

Put another way: if investment in something that is intended to contribute to someone's success (development of a program, purchase of a packaged course, buying a technology) isn't connected to a measurable result, then it shouldn't be created. Period.

How to Stop Wasting Your Company's Money

No one wants to be called out for wasting their company's money. Yet the same old assumptions and beliefs continue to fuel an industry as well as working practices. If you want an alternative, then this book is for you. If you're frustrated by the obvious ways in which people are wasting their time or working at odds with each other, by the constant stops and false starts, re-dos, and re-implementations, with no discernible progress, then you'll want to hear what we have to say. No one wants to live in a world of insanity.

In the remaining chapters, we continue to tell the story of a group of people who faced what seemed like an impossible challenge. They were saddled with insanity, and they found a way through, while achieving strong and clear results.

One thing to note about our story is that although the characters are fictitious, their situation is real. They represent a composite of the many people we have teamed up with to find success on previously thought-to-be-insane projects. We met a lot of people, learned about their roles, and had amazing opportunities to understand and empathize with just how insane their world had become.

Throughout the story, though, we'll be ourselves! You'll encounter Oxygen team members, and me, in this story. My role: keep unrelenting focus on business outcomes and empathy for people. It's this focus that guided and shaped a whole new way of working that is the basis for this book. You'll get to know our design and development team, who turned on a dime and became crazy productive, along with our composite client, using every imaginable modern device that technology had to offer, crossing time zones and traffic-jammed bridges alike. You'll read about what the results were like for the thousands of people who were affected by this work. And you'll experience through our story that the radical outcomes that have practically become table stakes for the world's most successful companies are human, creative, and simple – and entirely within reach.

This is a story about stopping the random acts and wasted investment, and adopting a whole new way of working. It's a story about learning and effecting change in – let's admit it – the fairly unsexy world of business, which is nevertheless where most knowledge workers spend the majority of their day. By the time you finish this book, you'll have:

◆ A new way to think and collaborate with your team, organization, and stakeholders

- ◆ A new way to build outputs
- ◆ A new way to work using a process and suggested strategies for getting started

Before we conclude this chapter, we recommend taking a minute to familiarize yourself with a list of terms used throughout the book. One of the most important steps to take in achieving Radical Outcomes is making sure everyone working together is using common terms with the same definition in mind.

A Glossary of Terms for Radical Outcomes

Audience: The people that you support who need to be successful in their role at your company. More specifically, we think of the people who are in front of your company's customers every day. Salespeople, customer service agents, field agents, business development managers, retail clerks, bank tellers, and many, many more.

Content: When we say "content," we mean subject matter, topics, and information – not how it looks or how it's rendered. Content can be in a variety of forms, including, but not limited to: articles, videos, courses, job aids, announcements, and memos. It can also be stuff that's in the head of a subject-matter expert. Whether we gather it, create it, or both, content is the source material for our audience(s).

Customer: Your company's customer, or the person representing the entity that purchases your company's products and services. Depending on the type of business, a customer can be a consumer, a head of a department, or a partner that sells your company's products or services.

Enablement Function: Group within a business, such as Marketing, Sales Support or Field Support, Learning and Development, Product Groups, or vertical Business Units, whose purpose (in whole or in part) is to provide support, content, or knowledge to their audience of customer-facing teams, and help them acquire the skills they need to be successful in their role.

Enablement Team: The people in place for an enablement function that produce stuff for the audience, comprised of different roles and responsibilities such as designers, facilitators, online developers, sales or field trainers. We use the term *Enablement Team* throughout this book; in lots of businesses, this team might be known as Sales or Field Enablement, Sales or Field Operations, Learning and Development, or Training.

Executive: The group within a business that steers the strategy of a business, and then provides sponsorship to the initiatives that are created to execute the strategy.

Outcome: A driver – a behavior, skill, or capability – that produces a specific, measurable business result.

Output: A tangible deliverable – a slide deck, a storyboard, an email, a video, a whiteboard drawing that supports a conversation.

Role: While we'll use the word "role" generally, we think of the role of the audience as a core building block for designing an experience. In this usage, it refers to the specific job that the audience was hired to do. Audience roles can be quite diverse, especially if you are in a large business that may have many, many types of roles that are customer-facing. Examples include Technical Seller, Solutions Architect, Account Executive, and Call Center Agent.

SME: Shorthand for subject matter expert. These are the people who have some kind of specialized knowledge that would be desirable for the audience to know and act upon in their role.

Stakeholders: The people who have an interest in the outcomes and results that are being driven by the audience.

■ ■ ■

In the rest of this book, we'll step through a series of approaches and ways of working that combine processes, principles, and mindsets that – in our experience – have resulted in extraordinary teams that are able to produce the radical outcomes that businesses require in today's complex and connected world. We start with that process in Chapter 2, "The Process: Don't Leave Home Without It."

We then discuss extraordinary teams, and ingredients for assembling them, in Chapter 3, Create Your Ensemble. In Chapter 4, "Let Go of What You Know," we discuss the need to work in a different way, which requires, well...letting go of what you know.

We then get into all the process steps in detail. In Chapter 5, "It's Business Outcome Time," you can read about how the new frame of reference – the key to effective collaboration – is the business outcome. In order to achieve Radical Outcomes, though, you'll want to read Chapter 6, "Putting Divisions Out of Business," which talks about how to work across those departments and functions that tend to operate in silos, but whose people have critical information for making your audience successful.

In Chapter 7, "The Experience Is Human," we talk about how to connect outcomes to your audience, by understanding their environment, how they work, and what can be done to measure their success specifically.

Chapter 8, "Why We Can't Live without Architecture," is all about just that: how architecture provides the structure to prevent the information overload and randomness that audiences must endure today.

Chapter 9, "Getting the Right Stuff," will share specific techniques for how to help your subject matter experts help you to help your audience. And then, in Chapter 10, "Not Your Average Design," we share ways in which design matters for your audience, and how to ensure you have the right design for the experience you are creating.

Chapter 11, "Knowing What Is Good Enough," shares a simple mindset that makes it easy to keep moving in an agile way when creating anything for anyone! And in a similar vein, Chapter 12, "Progress Is All That Matters," shares tips on how to make sure your stakeholders are aware of the hard work that makes an experience possible.

Finally, we send you on your way in the concluding Chapter 13, "Activate Radical Outcomes."

Before we do all of that, though, we need to talk about something that ties it all together: *the process*.

Are you curious?

The Process – Don't Leave Home without It

You must first know yourself, and then realize that since the process of practicing and learning continues throughout your entire lifetime without ever reaching completion, this process is all there is. The process is the thing, the only thing, and to the aspiring jazz musician, therefore, practicing is a way of life. Each musical experience is just practice or preparation for the next one. So, in a very real sense, it's all practice.
—Hal Crook, *Ready, Aim, Improvise*[1]

The pianist and the drummer walk to center stage and bow to the applauding audience. The energy in the air is one of anticipation. The pianist sits, waits for the applause to die down, looks at the few papers on his stand, and watches the drummer settle into his seat. He looks at the keyboard in front of him, then turns to welcome the audience, having sketched a few reminders about what to say. He addresses them as a host would welcome dinner guests, providing some tidbits of history and connection to the tune he's about to play. He makes a joke about the relation of the tune's title to the weather. Then they play.

The tune is familiar to the audience, yet as with most forms of jazz, one of the reasons this audience is here is because they want to see what this duo will do with it. Will they treat it as a slow, smoky ballad? Or change the meter into something complex?

They end up doing both.

The music starts in a familiar way, then the duo begins to interweave musical jokes, snippets of other tunes, and changes in rhythm. As they play, they laugh with each other, creating a new phrase happen and playing off it. They appear to be enjoying a conversation with each other, even stopping for an entire measure and resuming without skipping or leaving the safety of the beat. They've gone way off-book with their musical adventure – and yet the entire time, there is still no mistaking that the tune they are playing is "Autumn Leaves," a jazz standard from the 1940s. The pianist takes a turn and then –

"Olivia. Yo."

Jack knocked loudly on Olivia's office door, and her reverie, recalling last night's remarkable performance by her two musician friends, vanished into the air. "Need you in my office. Maya's on the line."

"Okay," said Olivia, standing up quickly. Olivia Chandler was in her late thirties, dressed in the standard business casual uniform of her workplace, but with a touch of artfulness – a handcrafted silver necklace of hammered medallions and an embroidered denim jacket that just slightly challenged the dress code. Her windowless office of standard-issue furniture was decorated on one wall with a large poster of Katsushika Hokusai's *The Great Wave Off Kanagawa*, with Mt. Fuji far in the background and three small fishing boats in the foreground, all dwarfed by the giant waves of the surf. On the other wall was a large white board.

Jack wordlessly turned and left, and Olivia gathered a notebook, her phone, and a pen from her desk. She followed Jack toward his office, jogging slightly to keep up, and then closed the door behind her. A conversation was already taking place on the speakerphone as Jack pressed the red button to unmute.

"I'm back," he said into the phone. "Olivia's here with me. Okay, I'm just going to recap here for Olivia's benefit..."

Jack spoke for a minute, summarizing, then Maya interrupted him.

"Guys. You've got 10 weeks to build it. I don't care how you do it; just make it happen. We're going to hire the first wave in 10 weeks. And you can't produce the stuff you normally do – I don't know how to put it other than bluntly – these people have to be ready to *do* their job."

The words swam around in Olivia's ears like dull white noise. When Jack called her into his office, she'd thought it was going to just be one of his fake fire drills, one of the many things he'd do to stir people up and distract them. But this time it was different. For one thing, Maya was actually on the phone, and the directive was clear. For another thing, Jack looked really uncomfortable.

When the call was over, Jack looked at Olivia. "Alright then. We have ten weeks. I'll need a plan from you in three days."

Olivia skimmed the notes she'd scribbled during the call. "Jack, there's no –" then caught herself, and paused. She looked directly at him. "There's no way we are going to get this done by working the way we've been. We have to make some changes."

Jack shrugged. "I'm never out of my league with you around, Olivia," he said, in that way that made her cringe slightly. Why did he have so much trouble being sincere? "What do you propose?"

"You need to let me run the process. Not whatever process we've randomly been doing. We're going to need to break it down..." She stopped. It was never a great idea to share all of what she was thinking with Jack. She needed time to gather her thoughts.

"I'll schedule some time for us tomorrow to review an approach."

"Three days," he said, with a challenging glint in his eye.

"I get it. Three days." She opened the door to his office and stepped out. "Talk to you soon."

To Conquer Random Acts...

When it comes to making your audience successful, we are willing to bet that in your organization, there are lots of stakeholders clamoring for *more stuff*. More leadership training; more courses on negotiation; more time management training for agents; managers should be able to coach, *and* do everything else in their job. Everything is expressed in terms of *more, better, faster,* or *should*.

In fact, we see a lot of use of the word *should* on the part of everyone except the person at the end of the line who is trying to be successful at their job, be they an agent, salesperson, soldier, or caretaker.

So how do people in a business agree on what can be connected to an outcome and what is nice to have? How do you get real about what's in and what's out, when it comes to creating stuff for the audience?

Our answer is: there's a process for that.

In all of our work with clients, we've had to have so many conversations about what to create and how it will help. We've had to be maniacal about clarifying assumptions – getting stakeholders to speak up and explain *why* a piece of content or concept is critical – that before we knew it, we'd developed a process. A way to create something as simple as a single presentation, or as complex as an entire global 90-day onboarding program. A way to ensure that the information is consumable; that the end outputs are easy to update in micro-iterations, and therefore have longevity; and that cuts through all the noise rather than contributes to it, because it's connected to an outcome. It's a way to take a team from envisioning the outcome, all the way through creating outputs so that the audience can *consume and engage with an experience* rather than *receive information one way.* Imagine having a process to create that, instead of sending yet another group of people through a training that's long been ineffective.

We have that way. With it, we produce Radical Outcomes.

The Process behind Radical Outcomes

The process behind Radical Outcomes is a series of structured stages that allow for fast, iterative progress. It's an organizing construct to help envision, guide, create, and update workable solutions for people that need to do something differently, or need help to succeed. By collaborating with stakeholders, understanding customers, and empathizing with your audience – we say, "Meeting people where they're at" – we can create repeatable, scalable, and measurable experiences and journeys at work.

Remember Olivia's jazz reverie at the beginning of this chapter? Some people may think that jazz and improvisation is all made up on the spot. Perhaps you've observed people doing something at a high level of performance, whether it's jazz or basketball. It almost seems as if they are communicating telepathically and doing something akin to magic.

It's not magic, though. What's happening behind the scenes, and the way high performing teams interact with each other, is actually highly structured. The choices musicians make during performance are governed by both foundational organizing constructs in music (such as harmony, melody, and styles of jazz) and by their own virtuosity (ability to access the complex language of their instrument). Without these structures, musical improvisation would sound like sheer cacophony. It would fail to engage the audience. Seasoned jazz musicians internalize the structure, reinvent and represent their take on a tune, and even manage the energy of the audience, drawing them in patiently, giving them just enough familiarity and just enough variation so that they want more. They make subtle notes to themselves on the fly – brush the snare drum here, wait to resolve that chord here – lending their own individual flare, yet never stealing the whole show. And even if someone in the ensemble heads in a new direction on stage in front of a crowd, everyone is able to stay in sync.

What's amazing about this is: musicians don't get to this level of performance by spending all of their time in a practice room by themselves. While individual practice is important for one's own virtuosity, musicians also have to work together and follow a process in order to credibly perform onstage together. They have to decide what the overall theme of their program will be, based on their audience. They have to determine what kind of environment or venue they'll be in – outdoors? Large stage? Café? They have to come up with a logical order – slow tunes to start, then end with exciting, upbeat stuff? Or mix it up a little? Then, they need to put it all together through rehearsing, deciding who plays what, and trying out different things to see what works best. Perhaps, if it's a brand-new program, they do a few trial performances in small venues. Only then are they really ready to take their show on the road, so to speak.

Such is the case as well for teams at work who are creating Radical Outcomes. We discuss the principles behind creating that team, in Chapter 3, "Create Your Ensemble." First, this chapter provides an overview of the process behind Radical Outcomes and puts those steps into a repeatable structure that can expand or contract depending on the scope and complexity of the outcome. The process is remarkably similar for creative endeavors of all shapes and sizes.

But to do all this, you'll need to shift your mindset, as we discuss in Chapter 4, "Let Go of What You Know."

Step 1: Envision. The first step to create something relevant, not random, for your audience, is by working with stakeholders to envision the specific business outcomes they are looking for. We work with all of our stakeholders to identify desired business outcomes. What's the future state that we are working toward? How will it be measured? This is covered in Chapter 5, "It's Business Outcome Time."

Step 2: Environment. Creating a great experience for your audience means that you need to factor in who they are, and their working environment. These considerations need to be factored in so that Radical Outcomes can be translated into something that's easily accessible and relevant. Working with stakeholders (using the mindset covered in Chapter 6, "Putting Divisions out of Business"), you understand the role and time frame you're creating for, and which skills and capabilities drive success (Chapter 7, "The Experience Is Human"). Together with stakeholders, you'll define what success looks like first, before creating any content. You'll establish design principles so that it's clear what "good" looks like (Chapter 10, "Not Your Average Design"). You'll factor in the time that your audience really has available, for what type of interactions. And you'll agree on the measurements that show business results – not just whether people attended, or liked the facilitator.

Step 3: Architect. Architecture in this sense simply means a structure that is the opposite of random. For this high-level view, we organize what people have to *know* and *do* to achieve the desired outcomes, and what is essential at the stage of the role they are in. For complex creations like onboarding experiences, which can span a 90- or 120-day period, this structure is encapsulated in a core artifact called an Experience Blueprint. In the blueprint, Radical Outcomes are translated into measurable objectives that can be achieved over time (Missions) and the sequences of interactions (Episodes) that cumulatively support the missions. The Experience Blueprint represents the end-to-end experience;

and together with the design principles you've agreed to, will drive the design, build, and activation of the experience. More about this in Chapter 8, "Why We Can't Live without Architecture."

Step 4: Design. Ah, design. It means so many different things to different people; so we also spend all of Chapter 10, "Not Your Average Design," on it. To achieve Radical Outcomes, the Design stage is about getting two things right: content and concept. Getting the content right means partnering with subject matter experts or agreeing on the content source to develop the most accurate and relevant content for the outcome. Nailing the concept means working with creative resources in an agile, iterative process to develop storyboards and draft materials, in accordance with agreed-upon design principles, and figuring out together how to make the content digestible and engaging. And, lest you wonder whether a storyboard is really necessary for what you create, we believe that storyboards are sorely missing in the workplace.

Step 5: Build. It might seem obvious at this point, but in the build phase, you build that which was designed. This can mean different things, whether a presentation or an entire experience. The more complex the build, the more stuff there will be to iterate, get feedback from user acceptance testing (UAT) groups, maintain frequent contact with stakeholders for sign-offs, and deploy to pilot groups. For a less complex build, such as a pitch meeting or an internal deliverable, we still recommend iterating in a similar manner, getting as much feedback as you can along the way (see Chapter 12, "Progress Is All That Matters"). Iteration is meant to be fast, and we borrow principles from Agile software development to get the team into a flow of working.

Step 6: Activate. In this stage, your audience consumes the experience. Whether it's a pitch meeting, business case, or an onboarding experience for new salespeople, this is where you see how it lands, gather more feedback, and then make updates as needed. Just as the quote implies at the beginning of this chapter, the work of maintaining an experience is never quite done – as the business changes, so should the experience. If it's well architected, updates are easy to do, revisions can be released on a

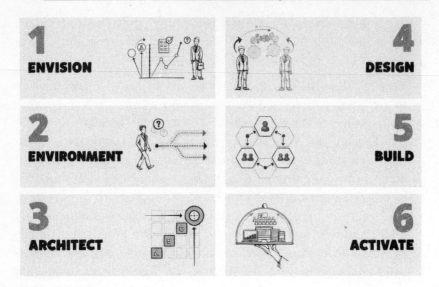

FIGURE **2.1**   The Process behind Radical Outcomes

regular basis, like software updates, and it becomes possible to measure the results of the experience. Figure 2.1 shows the whole process, end to end.

Your Audience Might Not Notice – But They Might Feel Different

Your audience may never really know that their experience is being architected for them, but they may come out of it thinking, "Wow. My company gives me what I need to be successful, and it's amazing how they insert it into my work environment, and make it easy for me to learn while doing my job!" Josh Bersin writes about learning in the flow of work in a recent white paper published by Deloitte: "Our research in 2015 found that among the 700+ organizations we studied, the average employee only has 24 minutes a week for 'formal learning.' People simply do not have as much time as they'd like to learn in a formal way, so this informal 'in-the-flow' work is just necessary for success."[2]

It is a validating feeling, and an important moment in someone's success at work: instead of working against the odds, they realize that they are part of something bigger, working to achieve larger goals with other people. This moment can be the point at which a company proves its value to its employees.

And perhaps more than prove value, this moment reveals that a company can be human. People drive the success of every business. They are behind the products, making the machines work, envisioning new assembly systems and workflow efficiencies, communicating with customers and each other. The process we use to serve audiences to drive Radical Outcomes, no matter where they are or what they do, is human.

Going Slow to Move Fast

The way the process is structured, time is invested in up-front work and alignment with stakeholders, as well as determining what content already exists, and what requirements will support the outcome.

Gathering all of these inputs and determining what is relevant for the audience at a particular point in time is difficult, and we've seen the objections by clients, or their sponsors, who say, "We don't have time to do all that up-front work. We need to build something *now.*"

We agree that the urgency is real. And we often will work with clients to put together both types of scenarios: one in which a quick win can be delivered, but might still be random; and another in which the work gets done right. Eventually, the random act can be designed into the architected structure.

Here's the thing. You can succumb to that pressure to build something now. After more than a decade of seeing people build things without architecture, and without taking the time to put themselves in the shoes of the audience, we believe that it's next to impossible to create something that connects with them. Which then leads to that stuff being ignored or put on a shelf. Going back to our first chapter, and the wasted investment – why would anyone choose that route? Contrast that with a process that invests more time up front to ensure relevance to the audience, to then make up the time by having what's needed to build at an agile pace, to then generate a measurable result – to us, it's a no-brainer that "going slow to move fast" is the way forward.

What's Agility Got to Do with It?

Agility is needed in the constantly changing world of work today: when unforeseen situations present themselves (a constant phenomenon these days!), you need to be able to change tasks to ensure you are still driving toward the key elements of the outcome. If you remain rigid on the actions set forth at the beginning of a project, you may run the risk of not meeting the desired outcome when things shift – and one thing is certain: *things will shift.*

Agile can mean a lot of different things to different people – specifically, those involved in software development. In that world, there's a manifesto for agile that means something specific to developers.[3] Our view of Agile leverages the quick-turnaround, iterative nature of the things you produce. Whatever you're creating, *it's far from perfect for the majority of the time that you'll be working on it.* In fact, much of the work will be captured in messy documents that can be hard on the eyes, aesthetically speaking.

The goal, however, in the early stages of the stuff you develop is not about making things look pretty. It's about getting the content accurate and the messaging right for the audience. It's about making sure you have multiple reviewers to provide feedback on the iterations, so that they catch what you might have missed. Seek to get feedback from as many different people as possible (who understand the outcome, of course) so that you feel confident about what is being produced, and that it will have the impact that you and your stakeholders are looking for.

That's what we mean by agility. It's the iterative manner in which you work. Working in this way means that you don't need to hold different things like content, design, or a concept close to the vest. You can work together to create the output that is going to be effective for someone else to do something that will drive a business metric forward. Think about the impact of this. Especially if you are in a large company, driving a business metric forward even just a few percentage points, and only producing that which has a direct link to that metric...that kind of a shift can make a huge difference for a company. Just how much of a shift?

It all starts with creating your ensemble.

Create Your Ensemble

How good can we expect to be if our best player is not our best teammate?

—Brad Stevens, Boston Celtics Head Coach

It's like conversation, thought Olivia, as the sounds of two saxophones weaving melodies around each other emanated from the Bluetooth speaker on the conference room table. The war room walls were covered in rolls of paper, and several open laptops were on the table. For a minute, Olivia was drawn in to the sound, marveling at the way the musicians responded to each other. But her enjoyment ended abruptly as the door opened, and Jack walked in ceremoniously.

"Where is everybody? I thought you said the team was working around the clock..."

"They went to get stuff for lunch, Jack," said Olivia. She looked at the room clock. "They should be back any minute."

He took a step back and brushed one of the laptops with his hand. The screen woke up and displayed a large spreadsheet projected onto the wall. The music was still playing, and Jack looked at the speaker. "Nice tunes. Who's playing?"

"Paul Desmond and Gerry Mulligan," Olivia said, even though Jack had shown no patience for understanding the nuances of the different musical genres that she'd put into the working session playlists.

"Okay, well," he grinned, "no time left to waste."

"No one's wasting any time, Jack. That," she said, pointing at the projection, "is all you need to know."

"What is that?"

"That is what we're using to track all the assets we're developing. I think at last count we had . . . around 987 assets going into 45 episodes for five missions."

"Since the contribution sessions? Wasn't that like a week and a half ago? Okay . . . that's impressive. I guess." He peered at the projection. "Though I can't make heads or tails of it all."

Not surprising. Why not ask: how are they doing that? But Olivia held her tongue. Being snarky to Jack would not help the cause.

"Form follows function," said Jack. Olivia mustered a smile at this phrase that Jack seemed to utter at every turn. She almost mouthed the words that followed. "Where there's a will, there's a way."

"Thanks, Jack. We're making a lot of progress. The team is amazing. Stop by anytime."

"Gotta run, Olivia. Keep up the good work," said Jack, and left the room.

Olivia sat back down and listened to the music, still playing over the speaker. She marveled at the way the two musicians were able to freely improvise yet stay structured so that the audience was still connected with them, as she was now, mesmerized.

She looked around the room, thinking about the way the team interacted with each other. Four weeks earlier, she'd been called into Jack's office and listened to Maya lay out the directive. Now, the team was assembled and had gotten through the hardest parts of the process. The designers and developers were in a rhythm, iterating within hours, then reaching out for feedback from each other, along with occasional input from an SME who just wanted to see how things were going. There was a rapport between the team players, a force of positivity, as Simon covered for Amalia's appointment, as Nimit checked in before going to a meeting to provide a business update, or when everyone took that short lunch break together. In other times, people would have multitasked behind their laptops or retreated to their corners. This was different.

It was like everyone was playing jazz.

■ ■ ■

Extraordinary teams. That's what this book is about, from the top of the strategy (the business outcomes), to the enablement of change (the experience). Propelling a business forward isn't alchemy or magic. It simply requires what we've called a new way of working within organizations, so that people receive what they need to change or to learn new things. Now we get to the heart of the new way of working: the extraordinary team.

While it can seem so obvious as to sound like a platitude, we all rely on others to accomplish major endeavors, whether it's parenting, performing, or publishing. And while it is true that some of our work requires solitude, focus, and our own individual capabilities that we bring, we've learned that much of our world is overrotated to burden the individual with Herculean efforts, rather than understand how a team of people can work together toward an outcome.

Our culture does tend to value the one hero or heroine. Most books have one author; there can only be one president of a country; we talk about having "one throat to choke" when we think about accountability; the Oscar goes to one Best Actor and one Best Actress. And while there are always opportunities to give kudos and acknowledgments to a team, it's hard to make the idea of "the team" the thing that's front and center, as if pointing out the people behind the Hero diminishes the romanticism of the accomplishment.

In reality, though, it's rarely one person who is able to achieve something all on their own (or if they do, it's at great expense, and it takes a long time, with many personal sacrifices). Even the artist Katsushika Hokusai, whose print hung on Olivia's office wall, relied on the talents and contributions of his engravers and printers to create his astonishingly prolific volumes of masterful prints. The examples of great achievements that we'll share throughout this book would not be possible without an extraordinary team.

While it's not romantic for those in search of a film-ready narrative, in reality – and in nature – teaming is the way things actually happen. Reality is much more an expression of many moving parts working in a symphonic balance toward an end, rather than the imposition of one willful component above the efforts of all other entities.

In essence, being on a team and getting help isn't weak, inglorious, or dilutive – it's actually what the smartest, most successful people do. These incredible successes are the mark of a group putting their personal goals aside and working to achieve something great.

Ensembles Make Sense at Work

Our working world provides countless opportunity and possibility to view things that might have seemed like obstacles or challenges as an individual, and instead view them as just part of what happens on a team. For example, you may know stakeholders who seem intimidating, either because they might disagree, or have broad responsibilities, or deep expertise in something. In reality, they are just part of your team. Without you, *they aren't going to be successful either.*

What's amazing about this opportunity is that it's how people actually want to work.

Unfortunately, barriers have built up over time based on the way our businesses *used* to work. Old ways of working, which we elaborate on in Chapter 4, "Let Go of What You Know," were great at automating repeatable processes. But when we spend all our time working in isolation, we also end up making assumptions about the ways other people work, or the way we are perceived.

When teams address these assumptions in the course of their work – for example, by identifying the working environment constraints for their audience, or defining design principles, as we discuss in Chapter 7, "The Experience Is Human," and Chapter 10, "Not Your Average Design" – they can find common ground and work toward their shared goals. When teams or individuals don't address these assumptions – "I'll never get funded for that" or "We don't do things like that here" – they lay the foundation for the barriers that have grown up inside of businesses everywhere.

Ensembles Don't Just Work Together – They Create

As its description suggests, extraordinary teams have something about them that helps them perform at a high level. It's as if they aren't just a team – they're an *ensemble.* We like this term because it makes us think of improvisation, jazz, and other creative arts that happen in the moment, or on the fly. And there's something about *how* an ensemble improvises or plays jazz that creates an experience for their audience that is intense, spontaneous, and engaging. When Olivia listens to the jazz duo, she is struck by how much unspoken elegance happened between the players. And the way they were so adept at managing what they wanted the audience to feel. They knew how to be in an ensemble.

In organizations today, the pace of change has become so rapid that teams have to have a mindset that is similar to the jazz ensemble. Unless a group of people is able to find a cohesive way of driving progress together, it becomes almost impossible to achieve a business outcome.

An Ensemble Is Collaborative, Not Competitive

In Charles Duhigg's book, *Smarter Faster Better: The Transformative Power of Real Productivity*, he tells the story of Julia Rozovsky, who attended the Yale School of Management in 2010 and had very distinct experiences with two different teams: her MBA study group, which was comprised of people with similar backgrounds and personalities; and a case competition team, comprised of a very diverse group of people from former military to a refugee program manager. The MBA study group was inherently competitive and highly stressful, where people were always ready to shoot down others' ideas or take credit for an achievement. They eventually dissolved and fell out of touch with each other.[1]

On the other hand, the case competition team generated many ideas, and grew as people began to hear about the creative dynamic and progress that was made. Moreover, its core members remain friends to this day.

Clearly, not all teams are created equal. Competition, possessiveness, and turf-sparring within a team undermine its ability to make decisions and move forward. But ensembles that cooperate and collaborate can achieve great work.

What Makes a Collaborative Ensemble?

What are some of the attributes that create Olivia's amazing ensemble, or the case competition team in Julia's MBA program?

As we'll elaborate, these attributes apply to both the team, and the management of the team.

COLLABORATIVE ENSEMBLES HAVE A COMMON GOAL OR MISSION

Alignment behind a common goal is one of the most fundamental components of success in an ensemble. The jazz duo had the performance of a specific tune as its goal; Olivia's team had to create a brand-new program from scratch in three months. Life is full of these interpersonal experiences with shared goals: our high school soccer team, the squad in the army, the orchestra we played in, the volunteer organization we spent weekends helping out. Shared experiences are so fundamental to human nature, they're part of our development from the day we are born.

COLLABORATIVE ENSEMBLES HAVE ROLE CLARITY

Imagine a baseball team with three pitchers on the field. Or a jazz ensemble with four drummers and one sax player. Those kinds of configurations don't really help to balance out the work that needs to be done. In an organization, teams also need clarity on how their roles fit together. What does the project manager do? Who makes the final decisions on design, or on content?

Additionally, in a dynamic environment, it's possible that people have to cover for one another. Just as the shortstop might need to tag second base, or the piano player needs to take over the rhythm while the drummer picks up the stick he dropped, sometimes ensemble members will play another role.

People need to know what's expected of them and need to know that it may be necessary to shift in and out of different roles to meet the outcome. How do they know what they are shifting to or from? From the outset, they have a defined role that is clear to both the individual and to the whole ensemble. This helps to drive accountability for the work, and makes it clear who to ask for what.

Part of the expectation within teams can also be this: life happens. If the Lead Designer is out for an emergency, or a vacation takes place, then someone else from the team might need to step in to lead review sessions.

To document role clarity, and have the flexibility needed to accommodate the unpredictable, we advocate having a structure in place that delineates and identifies different types of roles by the terms we introduce in Chapter 1, "The Why": stakeholder, customer, audience, and SME. This helps *everyone* on the team, including all stakeholders, understand "who's who in the zoo." Additionally, it can help to use the RACI (Responsible, Accountable, Consulted, Informed) model[2] for setting up a team and ensuring that it's clear when ensemble members might have to take on multiple roles, or how to call out who's doing what. The RACI construct is also helpful for providing specific feedback for someone's role.

Having clearly assigned roles is helpful, because when you want to step out of that role, you can declare it: "I realize I am the project manager on this work, but I have a thought on the design of that graphic – do you want me to give that feedback?"

What Are the Roles for the Process?

When we use the process to drive Radical Outcomes, we have specific roles on our team that are necessary for creating the architected experiences that help our clients.

Experience Architect

A skilled interpreter and facilitator. Experience Architects run stakeholder sessions and are responsible for assembling the sequence of missions and episodes that add up to Radical Outcomes. They also guide the construction of the experience by both helping to gather content and ensuring that what is created by designers and developers meets the needs of the audience.

Experience Designer and Developer

A talented communicator and wordsmith. Experience Designers and Developers have an eye for turning information into engaging activities, narratives, and interactions. They are responsible for creating storyboards for each part of an experience.

Creative Director

A visionary knowledge renderer. Creative Directors know how to bring an artistic view into the expression of business conundrums, and ensure there is a consistent, coherent look and feel that engages the audience.

Visual Designer

A producer of polish. Visual Designers take instructions from the Creative Director and bring information to life through agreed-upon mediums such as graphics, animations, or illustrations.

Experience Manager

A meticulous organizer and motivator. The Experience Manager oversees each and every stage of project work, managing backwards from the agreed-upon outcomes at the start of a project.

Role clarity and the RACI model are not particularly new, and in traditional project management, it is typically the area that most attention is paid to when considering how a team is assembled. But there's more to it than that!

COLLABORATIVE ENSEMBLES HAVE INTERPERSONAL CODES OF CONDUCT

One of the most important aspects of creating the ensemble is to set the context and expectations for how we work together. How do we act? How do we *not* act? Establishing a specific interpersonal code of conduct is both critical and requires specificity, or people simply won't understand what it means.

Ability to Say "I Don't Know" One of our favorite moments with a client was when she said, "I don't know the answer to this, so I am going to say something dumb so that someone else can say something better." Not having all of the answers, and articulating it, makes a team powerful in their ability to collaborate and brainstorm together to achieve an outcome. When we start with "I don't know the answer to this, here are some of my thoughts" it allows for others to chime in on their thoughts, and before you know it, you have come up with something that you may have never thought about before.

Authenticity Being authentic means recognizing that we are human, and that everyone on the team has strengths and weaknesses. When you can acknowledge those strengths and weaknesses, it frees you to work together more effectively: no need to pretend that you are good at something! And when the people around you understand this, they tend to help out, as well as ask for help in areas where you have strengths.

Transparency Being transparent can also lighten the complexities of juggling work and life. The reality is, people work, and people also have a life outside of work. We think of it not so much as "work-life balance" as "work-life integration," in which some of the things that have to happen in your life are communicated up-front so that others can cover and accommodate. For example, someone on your team might need to take one of their family members to an appointment once a week at a specific time. When the team is aware, they can work around it instead of that person carrying the burden of working during that time slot. When managers know in advance what is going on, their purpose is not to judge or tell someone they can't do something, it's to be able to plan coverage or set expectations on timing for a client, and that is much easier to do up front rather than right before a deadline or after a missed goal. Being transparent and proactive helps in so many ways to manage a highly effective team.

Asking for Help Ask people to reach out if they are working on something and are stuck on a concept or idea. A rule of thumb to consider: don't spend more than 15–30 minutes thinking about something before reaching out to a teammate and saying "I am stuck; will you talk this through with me?" Amazingly, that one small activity usually results in the person figuring out the path forward in far less time than if they had tried to figure it out on their own. This concept can be very intimidating, due to our fear of being wrong, as we discuss in Chapter 11, "Knowing What Is Good Enough."

In our culture's tendency to celebrate the singular hero, we are taught that proof of intelligence or capability rests in one's ability to figure something out alone. We don't believe this is true, at all. We believe that the combined wisdom of a team is *way* more interesting than of one individual. Having that belief allows us to ask for help, make shifts and advance to the outcome in a much more rapid pace than for those who choose to go it alone.

Yes, and...   In our work as an Oxygen ensemble, we've learned not to say "Yes, but..." when we're having a difference of perspective. We say, "Yes, and..."

Why? Because in terms of English grammar, our brains process the word "but" as a negation of everything that came before it. "Yes, but" indicates opposition, not collaboration. If you've ever done any theatrical improvisation, "Yes, and..." is one of the first techniques you learn for keeping the improvisation going.

We tend to hear "Yes, and" as a willingness to collaborate. That makes us more likely to listen to a different perspective, as opposed to feeling defensive. Try it out! It might feel strange at first – but after you do it for a while, you'll actually start to hear just how often the phrase "Yes, but..." is used in conversation. And you'll be amused.

COLLABORATIVE ENSEMBLES NEED A LEADER

In today's highly complex environments, where organizations and stakeholders are highly matrixed, change is rapid, and customer needs are shifting, we have also found that while there are several important attributes of ensembles, one element in particular is indispensable, without which an ensemble will fall apart under the weight of existing organizational structures and old ways of doing things:

The ensemble must have a leader. And that leader's primary responsibility is to *manage the energy of the ensemble.*

When we think about the leader of an ensemble, we don't necessarily think of it in hierarchical terms. And we definitely do not advocate the idea that leadership is synonymous with power, authority, or fear-based manipulation such as bullying, controlling, or shaming – those attributes have long been left in the dust as characteristics of poor leadership.

Remember Julia Rozovsky? She eventually went to Google's People Analytics group, and was involved in several of their fascinating research projects on the nature of team dynamics, including their much-publicized projects, Oxygen and Aristotle (the first project name is purely coincidental, but it makes us smile anyway!). In it, the researchers found that, while all high performing teams shared attributes such as feeling that their work is important, personally meaningful, with clear goals, the most important attribute was "psychological safety," first coined by Amy Edmondson in her dissertation on organizational behavior at Harvard.[3] We think of the term psychological safety as simply feeling that your leader "has your back."

Not only is it important, but it's also really up to leaders to create that sense of psychological safety in an ensemble. At the heart of every strong team is a leader who manages the energy of the individuals, ensuring a minimum of peaks and valleys, so that people can perform their best together.

Leaders Are Back-Havers and Orchestrators of Trust In many teams there are peaks and valleys of work. When people are aware of this, they know that they are going to have to work really hard in some places and less hard in others, expending different amounts of physical energy. There is also the energy that we bring to a team as individuals. Different people carry a different energy with them on a team, which can affect the dynamics of the ensemble.

Energy management of a team is an orchestration that happens across different interpersonal settings: *within a team, one on one, and across the process.* Because there is no one formula for energy management, the leader needs to navigate each of those settings and provide different aspects of the trust or psychological safety as needed.

Team Energy Management In a team environment, a leader needs to set up environments where people can show up, share their thoughts, disagree if necessary, or offer a different point of view and be heard. The leader or manager is there to de-escalate energy when it rises, or allow it to get intense if that is needed – and always bring it back to a place of productive energy. This is important if you don't want to burn out your people, yet consistently have a high production rate of quality outputs and high outcomes. Think of it as related to exercise. If you decide on an hour-long workout but give 100% of your energy in the beginning of the workout, you might have trouble finishing. But if you manage the major exertions of energy, but take time to rest in between intervals, then it's much more likely you'll maintain a good output level where you don't want to quit. With teams at work, it's the same type of management.

How does this happen? Here are some of the ways that leaders can manage the energy of a team:

- **Model the behaviors and the interpersonal code of conduct that are expected of the team.** Set clear codes of conduct – "this is how we act" and "this is how we don't act" – and then do just that. Don't declare one thing as valued, but then act against it. The consistency of your actions as a leader greatly influences how your team shows up, and how much management you have to do as a leader.
- **Provide clear, positive, specific guidance and context**. Leaders must constantly reinforce the outcomes and goals for the ensemble. They are responsible for articulating the *why* behind an initiative, and also connecting it to reality for the team. They set the context and expectations for how people will work together.
- **Figure out stuff *with* people, not *for* them.** Bring the team together and do the work together. Ask questions, make suggestions, listen to others, and come up with what is going to best serve the outcome. Do the work and model how it's done so that it continues when you aren't there.
- **Show up with respect and discretion for each team member.** When talking to one team member, never blame or talk poorly about another team member. Instead, keep calm, listen, evaluate and reflect on what you have been told. Weigh it against the values or code of conduct, then make a decision in accordance with the code of conduct. Then, simply keep moving forward.

One-on-One Energy Management　The leader also has to keep the energy intensity at a level that works for all individuals of the team. It's invisible work for most, and crucial for supporting productivity.

- ◆ **Know the strengths and weaknesses of the individuals.** Leaders connect an individual's strengths with their core responsibilities. They don't put someone in a position where their weakness will be detrimental to the outcome.
- ◆ **Provide care for the team members who need it.** If a team member has a personal issue, the leader is available to hear what's going on. As the leader or manager, you are there to help find a solution and bring the intensity of their energy back to something that is more balanced. You problem-solve together, and help the person return to a productive mindset.

Energy Management across the Process　The idea of energy management is also reliant on having a process that people know. Process is incredibly important, and at the same time, we've seen plenty of overengineered processes – meaning that people attempted to predict and prescribe so many details and actions that the process became more paralyzing than it was helpful. As one leader we interviewed said, "You have to have enough structure in the process to manage it, but enough flexibility to do what makes sense." We'll discuss the process that we use in Radical Outcomes, as the focus of our next chapter, "The Process: Don't Leave Home Without It."

Leaders Must Be Aware of the Self　All of these leadership qualities require awareness of the Self. If we have an issue or a personal demon that causes us to lose our cool or lash out in front of a team, we need to know where this comes from and deal with it. A leader doesn't get to drop the ball on issues of temperament – they always have to show up, even on the bad days. Sometimes this can be incredibly difficult – and it's part of what it means to be a leader.

In the next chapter, we talk more specifically about how different the new way of working will be – so different that it will require you and your team to let go of what you know.

Let Go of What You Know

It's what we think we know that keeps us from learning.
—Claude Bernard, physiologist

You've got 10 weeks to build it. I don't care how you do it; just make it happen. We're going to hire the first wave in 10 weeks. And you can't produce the useless stuff you normally do – these people have to be ready to do their job.

Back in her office with the door closed, four weeks before the team had coalesced, Olivia contemplated the discussion that she had with Maya and Jack over the past hour and a half. Three hundred new sellers. Another 300 technical salespeople. Ten weeks to build the program that would ramp them up to be able to handle customer calls and meetings about a complex array of products, customers, deal types, and processes. And Maya had flat-out said, *All the usual content has to be redone. It must be different. People aren't reaching quota. They're not staying in role long enough for it to matter for the company.* Jack had added, on mute, *The VPs are roasting us.*

Olivia knew what the world of sales was like in the tech industry. Ten years earlier, commiserating with her sales colleagues, they would complain. *Drinking from a fire hose. Trying to cram everything we needed to know into the first few weeks. Too much time spent doing administrative stuff, and not enough time actually talking to customers.* So when she needed to make a change from the life of a seller and decided instead to do what she could to make other sellers successful, she often found it astonishing how much information other people thought was okay to randomly throw at salespeople.

At the same time, this was a crazy directive. Why didn't anyone on Jack's team know until now that there was a strategy to hire all those sellers? Why was the concept of onboarding and training such an afterthought to all the other things that needed to happen to make the strategy succeed? If Maya did know, how come this was the first time that Olivia was hearing about it?

Olivia poked at the magnetic sculpture on her desk that she often shaped and reshaped when she was thinking pensively about an issue or problem. She thought about the people who had worked on the last onboarding program, before she joined the team – the ones who had created the stuff that Maya had trashed. No one had intentionally done bad work. But somehow it just didn't move the needle. What were the things that they did or didn't do that produced something that Maya didn't find helpful? As far as Olivia knew, most of the team of four to five people had never spoken to a customer, or heard a sales conversation, let alone ever filling a sales role. They didn't know what it was like to be a salesperson at Omen, Inc. Instead, they took all that complexity – the products, the processes, the information – and decided that *all* of it was important enough to cram into the program. Without asking anyone who actually had a point of view about what a seller might need to know in their first 90 days. No one actually realized that they'd designed a program with enough information to fill a whole sales career. What human could process all of that? And now it was out of date and had many different sets of intellectual property, depending on who created what. Olivia wasn't sure that they even knew what was in all of the stuff that had been created before.

I don't even know what I got for the investment made in what was created. Why haven't we seen results? We're going to do this over and do it right. Maya's words weren't angry, they were just . . . well, what someone would say when trying to drive results for a business.

Olivia took a deep breath. *You don't have to have all the answers right now,* she told herself. *We can figure this out. Life is like this, anyway.*

And she picked up the phone.

■ ■ ■

There are so many fascinating ways in which humans adapt routines that require a hundred little skills and moments of split-second processing to perform well. From solving algebraic equations, to becoming successful at work. When you first started learning something new, perhaps you felt challenged, thrilled, and tired whenever you found time for a break. Over time, the little things you learned become routine. Think about how you learned math as a kid: maybe even before you could read, you could count, first to 10, then 20, then 100. Somewhere along that path, you learned simple addition with single numbers. Some time later, you were doing multiplication tables, learning more complex routines, all the way through high school algebra, trigonometry and geometry. And if you liked all of that, maybe you studied calculus, pivoted into computer science or physics. But the entire experience of learning math involved that incremental increase, shift, and routine.

Consider the kinds of things people are asked to do at work, in spite of this reality. Entire businesses are having to transform the way they engage with customers. To make this happen, salespeople are told they need to have different types of conversations with entirely new audiences of buyers. Call center agents are expected to learn new internal systems and somehow navigate the impact to an increasingly demanding and informed customer base. And somehow, all of this shift and change is supposed to happen... immediately.

Think about an everyday bike commute in a big city. At every moment during these daily rides, cyclists are instinctively processing hundreds of inputs that they've learned to adjust to over time. A regular rider doesn't sit down and think through each of the tree roots they'll need to adjust for before their commute. They don't have a checklist about when to stand up in the pedals, when to pass on the left, and when to speed up into a turn. They just ride and react.

Now imagine what would happen if we reversed the gearing and steering one of those commuter's bicycles.[1] The entire skillset would change. The routine would be upended. They'd get to work late (probably using a different mode of transportation), feeling frustrated and challenged. Adapting to this new system is certainly possible, but many of the commuter's learned habits would have to be changed through consistent practice and focus over a long period of time. The cyclist would have to let go in order to accept the new inputs for commuting.

What's happening at the workplace today is that the gearing and steering is changing, and yet the mechanisms to help people adapt to that change are not emerging quickly enough to help. People like Olivia are being given directives to make other people successful, at a faster pace – because the business *has* to move that fast, because customers demand it.

Our Brains Want to Make It Easy

Our brains – the amazing organ that gives us consciousness, reasoning, and the incredible ability to process, shift, and analyze – actually don't like to work hard. In Daniel Kahneman's book *Thinking, Fast and Slow*, he studied the brain's capacity for decision making and analysis, and found that we tend to categorize information into different systems for different types of decisions.[2]

- ◆ System 1 is what we might think of as *intuitive*, where decisions, judgments and impressions come quickly, with minimal analysis, and using whatever information is on hand and immediately accessible in memory.
- ◆ System 2 is more *analytical* and thoughtful and must work hard to weigh and process different options, information, and scenarios.

An example of System 1 thinking is most people's instantaneous ability to add the numbers 2 + 2, where the information is learned, stored, and readily available for recall, and we can say with great certainty that the answer will be correct whenever the numbers are added.

System 2 tends to come into play for more complex or problematic evaluations, such as adding the numbers 25376 + 44365, or deciding which stock to buy or sell, or reflecting on how to share bad news in a kind way.

The issues between System 1 and System 2 arise when we become familiar with a way of doing things or making decisions so routinely that they become habit, accessible by System 1 whenever needed. When someone says "I was on autopilot," they are taking the things that they've learned how to do, and their brain is filing them into System 1 for easy access – because the brain wants to do as little work as possible for the circumstances presented. That our brains can do this is wonderful and amazing, and allows us to master musical instruments and perform brain surgery and land planes on the Hudson River during an emergency.

When it comes to changing what we do at work, however, System 1 gets in the way. Well-intentioned as ever, System 1 kicks in every day and immediately tries to provide answers, decisions, judgments, and interpersonal interactions to a world of work that has literally been turned on its digital head. It's why a grandmother who's 80 years old simply can't bring herself to use an iPad, even if it would mean connecting more often with her grandchildren. It's why Olivia's team was so blind to the program they'd created, which was about to be dismantled.

And it's why we feel so incredibly uncomfortable taking a step back and a hard look at the way we work and recognizing that just about all of it is a poor fit for our complex, shifting, digital workplace. For most people, letting go of our beliefs about most anything can be incredibly challenging. Letting go can be threatening; it can feel like we're admitting that we're wrong. And that's normal, too – our brains are wired to call up the easiest decision mechanism, and to defend *the way we've always done it* even if the facts suggest a new way to be more productive.

Just as Olivia took a deep breath before telling herself that she could figure it out, we also need to let go of the things that we think we know to be true. It's about giving System 2 a chance to work differently. And it's not just a "nice to have" – the future of work is here, and it needs you to change.

Change Is Preceded by Letting Go

Whether it's been expressly articulated or not, the expectations on each individual at work are shifting radically. People in Olivia's position are finding that the demands of the business, reflecting the demands of customers, are creating the need for work that has measurable impact. Every single person who receives a paycheck in a business is subject to the broad tectonic shift that is determining new criteria for what *productivity* means. For some, technology will overcome a human's ability to do certain kinds of work, and that person's job will be replaced by a robot. For others, technology becomes a tool to derive better, faster outputs from fewer people. Either way, expectations are shifting, and we – all of us – will sooner or later think about why we have a job, and how we do it.[3]

But how does it feel every day at work, this pressure to change?

Right now, if you're working in the old way, it feels like stress. Like piles of work on your plate. Like nothing is ever right in terms of the stuff you produce. Like the results are out of reach. Like you're a hamster running on a wheel with no end in sight. It's a rather existential dilemma, and in the scheme of things, probably not how most of us want to spend the minutes, hours, days, and years of our lives, which we can never retrieve or get back.

We have been in this situation ourselves, as well as many of the clients we work with, feeling as if the deadlines, requirements, and pressure to produce results are all adding up to an impossible mountain to climb. And we would agree, it's not possible – if you are working in the old way.

But there is a flip side, where productivity goes through the roof, where people are amazed at what's being produced, where a team works in a flow. It's hard work, to be sure, and when done right, it is also enjoyable work. And it's what this book is all about.

We have gone to many companies, brought in our way of working, and heard "that's impossible" and "it takes way more time than that" over and over again. Yet, over and over again, we've used the process, lived the principles, and achieved radical outcomes with clients. When Olivia makes her phone call, she's about to launch that new way of working. But the decision she makes isn't about picking up the phone, or deciding what to provide to Jack for a plan. It's far more fundamental than that.

Olivia decides to let go of what she knows, and is open to the possibility that other things can be true.

The Journey Begins

Learning a new way to work is going to be a journey for you and your teams – one that will be realized through incremental change and doing things slightly differently every day. If you thought that transformation would happen by reading a book, well, we can relate! In reality, just as with math, that's not how it actually happens.

Transformation can *begin* here. By the end of this book, you'll have had the chance to absorb and mull over the core concepts of the new way of working that we believe is the future way of working in a team, one that drives Radical Outcomes through doing. Then, as with any new thing you learn, it all depends on whether you action some or all of the ideas here and bring them to your environment and audiences.

Our approach is different from what you may have experienced in your organization. Depending on your organization, it may feel *really* different. Your culture and work environment might be more formal and hierarchical, or it may be more geared toward open discussion. Just as we describe in Chapter 1, "The Why," there are three altitude levels of people affected by the ways of working: C-level executives, who set the direction of the business; Leaders of teams who guide people toward the outcomes required for the business; and Teams who must make those outcomes happen through customers. Each of these three levels can respond to – and sometimes struggle with – change.

Part of the tension is how the old and the new are interwoven: a necessary part of reality. In Chapter 6, "Putting Divisions out of Business," we show how the old ways of working are not set up for cross-functional collaboration, and that organizations and individuals are often sealed off, or siloed, from each other. At the same time, shift can happen incrementally through people. To really understand the contrast, we need to dig in a bit more into that old way.

The Old Way and Why It Doesn't Work

A division VP prepares a justification for his annual budget. A research director assembles a case to get funding for an interdisciplinary study. Or – as in the case of Jack, Olivia, and her team – a group of people are suddenly on the hook to create stuff for new sellers to be quickly ramped into their role – and do it according to some vague new standard that it just "has to be different."

What do these all have in common? No matter what the thing is that's being created, the chain of enablement has a positive intention: drive a business forward through sales growth or achieve another form of results.

What happens when we start to really look at how we create these types of outputs? Where do our practices, habits, and knowledge actually come from? The answer is a bit alarming: many of the concepts we use at work today to engage, converse, produce, and develop are rooted in stale, decades-old theory. In some cases, we try to enable our people using methods developed during the Industrial Revolution! There is a lot of System 1 in play when we assume that how we work doesn't need to change, even as the world has changed around us.

In the mid and late nineteenth century, large leaps in our abilities to build and manipulate machinery allowed companies to scale far beyond cottage industries. Organizations grew alarmingly and needed more people to operate with and alongside machines to meet exploding customer demand. Often, workers needed a discrete set of skills and system of understanding to perform rote tasks quickly. To deliver these skills, employees were sat down in rows while concepts were explained to them, then sent to the factory floor to perform these tasks over and over again on assembly lines. Workers reacted to objects in various states of production, made the instructed inputs and adjustments, and repeated. Sometimes managers would ask machines and people to work faster, or longer. Sometimes machines would break down, and technicians would scramble to find, assess, and fix the problem. Promotions were offered to those able to work the hardest, the longest, as close to perfection as they could be.

That's what it was like to work in a textile factory in the 1870s.

Nearly 150 years have passed. And while there are still many jobs that require repetitive behavior, there are hundreds of thousands of new jobs that don't. It shouldn't be a surprise that what worked to run a mill at scale doesn't fit for knowledge workers, salespeople, and many others. Yet, think about the last meeting you attended, or facilitated. What language was used to describe decisions? What expectations did the participants have about what needed to happen? Were assumptions put out on the table and discussed, or did people nod, multitask, complain, or disengage?

We are seeing old theory and practice colliding with a world filled with people who know and demand more than ever before. This is, in part, creating the high-stress world we work in. We wish we could tell you it's overly dramatic, but unfortunately it's a daily reality for too many of our clients. What's the source of the friction?

Many businesses have unknowingly set up their functions in sales support, marketing, enablement, learning, and even R&D, to work in old ways, based on the assumption that everyone knows what needs to happen between setting a strategy and carrying out a task. Just let System 1 handle it, right?

In the digital age, however, so much has shifted and created a vast set of assumptions between the strategy and the execution of work toward that goal. How do you see implementing the strategy? How will you measure success of the strategy? Who is this impacting? Who else do you need to work with to make this strategy really work? Do you know enough about your customers to implement this strategy, or is there more research that needs to be done?

In the old way, the norms that are typical for teams, as well as entire functions, can be characterized as: wait for requests to arrive, then scramble to produce outputs on their own, often trying not to bother the stakeholders who made the request in the first place. The most challenging aspect of this behavior is that it is undetected by those who are doing it, and unmeasured by those who are in leadership positions. So the behavior continues in order-taking mode, often for years or decades.

Assessing the Big Picture

Because there aren't meaningful measurement systems in place, it's impossible to manage until someone shines the light, like this client did:

When I first arrived as the VP of Learning and Development, with a remit to transform the whole function to have a bigger impact on our agents, the first thing I did was to assess the lay of the land. I visited call centers, interviewed agents, talked to front line managers and trainers. And you know what I found? Sixty-five percent of the content that we were creating to train agents was being reworked.

Now we have a process in place to have the conversation with the call center leaders about what kind of measurement they are driving, and how the learning we create is contributing to that.

This systemic dysfunction probably sounds quite familiar to you. We know that whenever we ask people about their working environment, they describe themselves as a character in the scenarios our client portrayed. They say, "That's my company times three." And then, when we think about that individual person, here are the things they often don't see about the way they work.

They shoulder the entire burden of creating something alone, believing that they have to come up with all of the answers. By taking on that burden to create something alone, despite degrees and experience, they struggle to make the output relevant, and don't perform the necessary steps to validate its relevance to the audience. Because of this, even the most well-intentioned attempts to help the audience result in random acts or Herculean efforts that turn out to be Band-Aids, not real or lasting solutions.

This is happening across industries in the modern world. Does it sound familiar to you?

Good News – There's a New Way

Let's shift our focus now to sharing a new and sustainable way forward. And this way forward is what the rest of this book is about!

Remember what we wrote earlier about what it could feel like to work in a new way and be really productive? While it doesn't necessarily make work easier, and it requires a willingness to confront enormous complexity, it's also meaningful. Imagine an environment where those around you are supporting you, and everyone on the team is galvanized around building success together. We aren't kidding. It's possible.

First and foremost, in the new way, you get to play a different role. Instead of being an order taker, or shouldering the burden of deciding in a silo what people should learn to be successful, here's what we're going to see happen to Olivia and her team – and to you.

Engage with people differently. Teams, stakeholders, sponsors, and even people who disagree with you, all have a common purpose and can figure things out together.

Don't assume you have a solution. Solutions are great for things that have already been figured out. But in our complex world, which behaves a lot more like cloud computing than a factory floor, maybe there isn't an easy or apparent solution. Maybe it's more helpful to think about the issue with other people, and let the solution emerge.

You don't have to make it perfect. We have a saying, "Don't let perfect be the enemy of progress," and we spend a whole chapter talking about this: Chapter 11, "Knowing What Is Good Enough." Perfection – or coming close to it – is great for organizations with no shortage of money or for situations that require lots of polish. But even a process that is polished is still not perfect – and it's much harder to change. You need to be agile. And you need to be relevant. But not perfect. Letting go of the notion of perfection, we have found, is a big relief!

In fact, you'll learn in later chapters that no matter what you're creating, relevance for your audience matters far, far more than most other things. And when you work with your audience in mind, you can now add this new cool thing: render relevancy into an experience that is easy to consume. For us, this makes all the work worth it.

We like to think that the sum of our parts becomes greater than the whole. And the lynchpin of that New Way is a simple word that is packed with meaning: an *outcome*. When Olivia makes her phone call, she'll be asked a lot of questions about this word. And it's what the next chapter is all about.

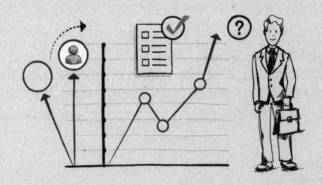

ENVISION

It's Business Outcome Time

We talked about a computer on every desk and in every home.
—Bill Gates[1]

"Hey, Juliana, it's Olivia. I'm so glad I caught you. Do you have some time to talk?"

Olivia paced the small perimeter of her office, speaking on her Bluetooth headset. Her white board, on the opposite wall from her computer, was filled with lists and a calendar in black, green, and blue.

There was a silence as Olivia paused to listen to Juliana on the other end of the phone line. Then she took a deep breath. "Okay, let me start with this. I'm just going to talk at you and you can interrupt me, alright?

"The deal is this. You know Maya, the VP of Vertical Tech that we met in the working session that you led? Okay, well, she is in charge of the A&D division sales teams for the Americas. It stands for Aerospace and Defense."

Olivia took a swig of water from the bottle on the desk.

"So, she was called into a meeting of all the regional directors, and also the RTF . . . that's the Role Task Force, remember . . . to discuss the results of the productivity study. The one I told you about – run by CGG. Sorry about all the acronyms. That's the consulting firm that spun off from the big one we were working with. They got the data

53

back and it's pretty scary – attrition from role, not attaining quota for nine months, there's some other stuff in there. So Rivers is not happy, and he is basically asking all the VPs and their regional directors to shape up their game by the end of the next fiscal year. Right, in about a year."

Pause.

"Well there are two scenarios with her. She's got a lot of new hires coming in as the result of that demo center opening up in Reston. I mean, they aren't all going to be located in Reston, but they have to be able to bring an engineer in and show some of the embedded OS functionality... sorry, I got a little technical on you there. But, yeah, she also has a bunch of technical people who aren't performing. Hang on, someone's texting me."

She typed quickly with her thumbs and put her phone down. It buzzed, she picked it up, and thumbed some more.

"Okay, sorry. My kid is locked out of the house – had to tell her where the key is. Where was I? Oh, so then she goes to Jack and basically says, what are you going to do for me here? So Jack and I had a call with her this morning and... yeah." She listened.

"Right, it's just like what you and I had talked about before, this team never measured anything for the business. And when Karina – you know, the person I replaced – was working with that group, she just sat on those requirements for like two months!" Olivia paused.

"Karina was like a deer in headlights. I think... she just didn't know what to do. Jack totally had a heads-up months ago that this might come down. But she didn't do anything about it. And so maybe for him, it was out of sight, out of mind? I don't know. I don't get it..."

Another pause as Olivia listened. She looked at the whiteboard. "Hang on a minute, I want to write this down. I need to erase my board."

Olivia's conversation continued for the next 30 minutes. She erased, talked, and scribbled quickly on the white board. "Okay, let me just read back to you what I got. I'll send you a picture, too. Here goes:

"No clear onboarding program exists for these roles. Did you get that?

"Okay, next, she talked about how they received like 50 emails on their first day about required training. Ugh. Yeah, she wasn't so friendly about that one.

"They're not doing any of the training because it's too confusing.

"Ramp up is taking longer because they are doing everything on their own and it's not... what did I write there? Optimized."

Olivia looked at the board for a minute. "Okay, so it does read a little negatively. I mean, people do seem to like our team... yeah, I know, that doesn't translate to much..."

She continued, "Okay, I think the final one is that the content is too complicated and there's too much of it for the new hires." Pause.

"Yes. Okay, thanks for keeping me on track. The outcome. So what they want to do is cut the ramp-up time for them to achieve quota. I had to really go back and forth with Maya to get that out of her. It wasn't actually clear.

"I mean, it *was* clear that's the result they want, but it wasn't clear that it needed to be articulated to our team. Like, she even said, 'This isn't the kind of information I usually discuss with Jack's people, it just didn't occur to me. His team usually comes to us and asks what courses we want, or we go to them when we just want to see what stuff they have.' I guess I was the first person to ask her questions about the results she was trying to drive."

"Okay? Think about that, and let's talk again tomorrow. I have to give a plan to Jack on Thursday. I know... this is crazy... okay, thanks."

Olivia hung up the phone, took another swig of water and looked at her whiteboard. She stepped forward and drew a large red box around one phrase: REDUCE TIME TO QUOTA.

She looked at it briefly, then erased part of the red box to add another phrase: STAY IN ROLE LONGER.

And then wrote on top of the box: THE OUTCOME.

Then she put the cap on the marker, and walked out of the room, down the hall to Jack's office.

■ ■ ■

In a 2008 interview with *The Telegraph*'s Claudine Beaumont, Bill Gates reflected on his aspirations for Microsoft. "When Paul Allen and I started Microsoft over 30 years ago, we had big dreams about software," recalls Gates. "We had dreams about the impact it could have. We talked about a computer on every desk and in every home. It's been amazing to see so much of that dream become a reality and touch so many lives. I never imagined what an incredible and important company would spring from those original ideas."[2]

Notice he did not say, "We talked about building lots of computers."

What Gates and Allen did was to focus on the outcome.

Customers, Strategy, and Execution

In Chapter 4, "Let Go of What You Know," we conclude by introducing the word *outcome*. As we discussed, today's workplace contains a proliferation of random things created for your audience. Through the well-intended purpose of educating, illuminating, or teaching a new skill, people are now deluged with information in amounts that no human can be expected to process. How do you find a way to cut through all that content, and hone in on what's most important? In this chapter, we focus on the idea of focusing on an *outcome* and working backwards from there.

Outcome. It sounds so simple to boil it down to one word, but what does it actually mean? To answer this question, and to illuminate why outcomes are so important, let's look at this through the lens of your company's CEO.

How does a CEO decide on what investments to make in their business? Put simply, they are doing what they think is needed in order to shift and adapt their business to the changing needs of customers, while also factoring in shareholders and their own employees. They then task their own leadership with goals and directives that are intended to deliver results. Yet businesses are struggling; the top companies – in terms of market capitalization – that used to dominate their respective industries have been replaced by technology companies, several of which didn't exist 10 years ago.[3]

Why is there such a breakdown between the strategy and results that a CEO is looking to drive and the work of their people to execute that strategy? It's not just about checklist manifestos or "getting stuff done" in a disciplined way. As we describe in the previous chapter, much of what happens between the CEO's vision and the work done to carry out that vision ends up in what we call "random acts" of creating stuff.

Random Acts Happen because Change Is Happening

As we discuss in Chapter 1, "The Why," the demand for better customers experiences has caused major disruption in every business and every industry, even for businesses that don't directly serve consumers. Whether it's doing more with less, bringing better products and services to market, or making major shifts in the way sales or service people show up for conversations with customers, the transformation involved is not optional. For many businesses and their shareholders, change isn't happening fast enough. Urgent directives ensue, with calls for action across all of those functions we mention in Chapter 1, to better support the audience:

◆ Product groups begin creating more materials for the audience to use in selling.
◆ Marketing groups begin creating more campaigns and messaging.
◆ HR and learning groups start creating more skill development courses.
◆ Sales and customer service organizations introduce more tools, re-do territories, and implement new selling methods.

And the Executive sponsors are funding all of these initiatives.

None of these activities are necessarily "wrong" by themselves. Some might be helpful in isolation. Each leader in each area is doing what they think is the right thing to support the audience. But, because everything is urgent, important, and must be executed right away, no one is checking in with the audience to see if it's actually helpful for them. The random acts that are created by these groups in response to the executives' strategy are actually undermining or canceling out any real benefit.

The Outcome Is the Thing

In her phone call, Olivia had to respond to a lot of questions about the business outcomes that Maya and her sponsors were looking to achieve. People at Maya's level and above are trying to make investments that move the needle against those outcomes. Yet those executives still struggle to understand what they are getting for that investment. Even though Maya's peers said they liked Jack's team, they also didn't feel like they could count on them to produce what was needed. And Jack had not been successful at showing a result that Rivers, Maya, and that level of executive would really care about.

We explored this problem with many clients and observed the lack of results – and the proliferation of random acts – at just about every business we encountered. Using the same grouping of organizations that we introduce in Chapter 1, "The Why," of Executive leaders, Enablement team, and the Audience of customer-facing people, here is the pattern that we found after five years of research and conversations with leaders across different disciplines in charge of driving business metrics:

> *CEOs and other executives (CFOs) are not seeing the connection between their investments in enablement, the work that's happening to create programs for the audience, and the results generated by that work.*[4]

What's the missing link in making that connection? To further investigate this question, we did our own research to compare and contrast high-performing organizations (HPOs) with low-performing ones (LPOs) and found across the board that HPOs tend to execute one task very well:

> *High-Performing organizations measure the impact of the stuff they create, and connect it to a business outcome.*[5]

Here's what that means. With so many random acts of creating stuff, who gets to determine what the audience needs to know or do? Is it the squeaky-wheel VP who runs the call center in Minneapolis, or the head of Operations group who seems to have so many allies? Do we just create stuff because "my boss said to do it?"

What if you could authentically cut down on creating stuff that isn't business critical? And at the same time, you could connect the dots between the funding you receive, and the impact of what you *do* create? When Olivia did her phone call, she relayed that the one thing that was difficult to extract from Maya was the desired result of reducing time to quota for new hires. Not because the desired result wasn't clear; it just wasn't the type of conversation that typically happened between Maya's leaders and Jack's group.

We find this disconnect fascinating. What is going on there?

To answer this question, we then looked at what was going on at the Enablement level of the organization. We found that many organizations actually *do* agree on measurements; the problem is that the measurements don't really say anything about business impact. Instead, they might measure "how many people went through sales onboarding," or "who attended a session about a new process," – things that check the box, but don't reveal whether that experience actually helped someone do their job better.

To illustrate this, Figure 5.1 shows the types of things that organizations measured when it comes to learning in the workplace. On the left are measures that represent business impact: retention, time to proficiency, percentage of quota attainment. And only 18% of our research base said they measured these factors! Contrast that with the measures on the right, characterized by attributes such as "audience reactions," and measured by 59% of our research base. Herein lies the disconnect: If the Enablement teams aren't measuring something with business impact, there's no way for the Executive level to know what they are getting for their investment.

What's really missing in that translation between strategy and execution is the ability to stay focused on the *only common element that connects the two domains*: a business outcome.

What we're proposing is a way of working where, no matter the task or the role, people are able to drive business results because they see how their work impacts the company's goals. Being able to draw the connection between one's work and a real business impact isn't just what Executives want to see, it also results in higher employee engagement and performance.

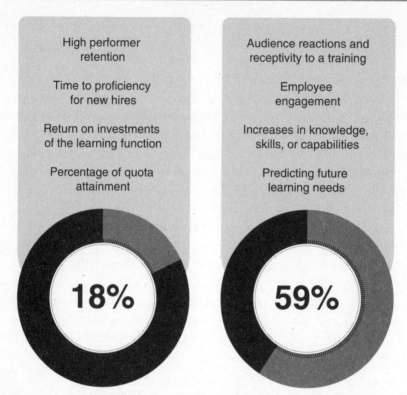

FIGURE 5.1   Organizations Aren't Measuring Business Impact of Enablement
Source: "Working in a New Way: Modeling the Human Side of Organizational Success," Oxygen, June 6, 2018, https://oxygenexp.com/wp-content/uploads/2018/06/Working%20in%20a%20New%20Way_Web.pdf.

"When environments provide and people seek out interesting, meaningful and challenging tasks [clearly related to business outcomes], individuals in these situations are likely to have... manageable difficulties and... optimal states."[6]

That connection between what you are helping the business to achieve, and the work you do, can be muddied by the fact that there are so many random activities. Chances are that you produce tons of outputs, based on the expectations of your job description. Do you always know the outcome you're driving toward? Or how that outcome affects business results?

What Happens When You Lose Sight of Outcomes

We have often run into situations where random things are created because no one is focused on the outcome. One lead designer for an onboarding program decided that the audience needed a course on "stress management." Why? He later told us "Well, the people I've spoken to are all, well, stressed out!" The problem with this reasoning is that it wasn't tied to any success metric for the role – and was a moment in time during a large merger, where stress was probably running high. How would this program be explained to an executive?

What's an Outcome, and What's an Output?

Here is the deal. There is a *big* difference between an *outcome* and an *output* (see Figure 5.2).

In our work we found that these two ideas can be misrepresented. The "stuff" we create does not, in itself, constitute an outcome for the business. How can it? Every email, meeting, presentation, or experience that we create is just one thing by itself. Of course, we have the ability to connect all of those things together, and often do. And, if we are able to really stay focused on something that's common for everyone involved, then those outputs become vehicles to drive the desired outcome.

Outcomes keep everyone focused on what's most important for your organization and provide a way to measure whether you've achieved a desired result. Put another way: if you can't connect your work and your outputs to a measurable result and outcome, should you even be doing it at all?

An outcome-based mindset leads you to focus on results first, and outputs or actions second. Identify the desired business result(s) first, and then you can identify the tasks necessary to achieve them. A salesperson for a large technology business, who is accustomed

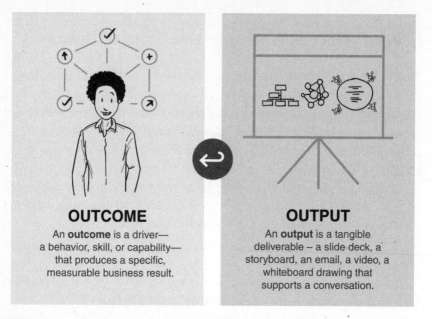

OUTCOME

An **outcome** is a driver—
a behavior, skill, or capability—
that produces a specific,
measurable business result.

OUTPUT

An **output** is a tangible
deliverable – a slide deck, a
storyboard, an email, a video, a
whiteboard drawing that
supports a conversation.

FIGURE 5.2   The Difference between an Outcome and an Output

to orchestrating deals with a Chief Information Officer (CIO), would head into their first call with a CIO thinking about how to have a conversation about the CIO's role and the challenges and pressures she is facing, so that she finds value in the conversation and agrees to another meeting to explore how his company can help her. To be prepared for that outcome, the salesperson has to be conversant in her business. He'll have to do some planning to learn about what other opportunities or contracts are already in play between the two entities. He'll need to research where some of the challenges might be coming from, by reading annual reports. Some of those steps may lead to outputs – a discussion document, a whiteboard.

But the outcome – agree to another meeting, to move a potential opportunity forward, to reach a shared vision of how his solutions can address her problems, is always what that salesperson has in mind. Focus on the wrong thing – such as selling her something she doesn't need, just to make a sale; or spending too much time talking about his company or products – and she'll become annoyed and feel like her time is being wasted. Or she'll delegate the meetings to people on her team, and take herself out of the loop, causing more work for the salesperson. The outcome then becomes unreachable.

When you are outcome-based, you always have the bigger picture in mind. *Always*. You make decisions about outputs and tasks based on whether or not they move you forward toward the outcome.

Thinking in an outcome-based way can be an individual mindset, but it also can be a group mindset. It can even be an organizational or functional mindset. We believe strongly that having an outcome-based mindset is what makes all the difference in the work we do. The specific, measurable outcome becomes the north star that always helps you navigate. In the salesperson example, the outcome is to close a large deal by arriving at a shared vision of how his company's solutions can help this CIO. For Bill Gates, it was a computer on every desktop.

When you know what the clear measurable outcome is, you then know what to focus on and what to de-prioritize. You can keep yourself and your team focused on all of the piece parts – the outputs – that will enable the outcome and you can explain this to anyone who asks about the rationale for your team's actions and outputs.

Not Just Any Outcome: Radical Outcomes

When Olivia has her phone call and describes the outcomes that her stakeholders want to drive toward, she's not yet aware that she's about to set up a way of thinking and working that is going to be radically different. There *is* something radical about what's being asked of her: the directive to re-do an entire onboarding program, so that hundreds of new hires would hit their quota *and* hundreds more would stay in their role longer, all to be delivered in a very short time frame. To achieve that kind of radical result means a major change in how she and her team will work.

It's arguable that there are many types of outcomes one could drive toward in business. Our salesperson example given previously shows outcome-based thinking for a single large deal.

And while a single large deal is great for that salesperson and that CIO, there's nothing radical about such an isolated example. By itself it doesn't produce a major business impact.

But what if someone could help 50 salespeople learn how to think and plan the way he did with the CIO? And 50 salespeople started closing large deals, repeatedly and consistently, because they knew how to have valuable conversations with their customers? Or 500 salespeople?

The directive that Maya received during the executive meeting at the beginning of our story wasn't simply made up on a whim. Deliberate research had been done to show that the productivity of the sales teams had a lot of room for improvement, and that the technical sellers were struggling to move opportunities forward. All of these aggregated factors had rightly made the executive team extremely anxious to take corrective action. When they called the meeting, it was to bring together a cross-functional group of executive level stakeholders who would all be enrolled to achieve the outcome. There was a result that they were looking to achieve, and they knew that it would take time – across multiple waves of new hires – to get there. This all led to the pressure on Jack to deliver something as soon as the first round of new-hires showed up for day one.

Radical Outcomes Are Tied to Complex, High-Stakes Initiatives That Yield Tangible Results

Here are the basic criteria that differentiate a Radical Outcome from something that is just run of the mill.

EXECUTIVE LEVEL, CROSS-FUNCTIONAL STAKEHOLDERS ARE INVOLVED

To drive change in the business where the impact is truly felt by customers, executive sponsorship is needed, usually because there will be so many different groups involved in working toward the outcome that it requires someone at the executive or business unit level of an organization to provide the endorsement of the initiative.

RESULTS ARE ACHIEVED OVER TIME

Every executive wants change to happen "yesterday," yet even so, it takes time for an organization to adapt and change, especially when the change itself is radical. Urgency defines the need for these changes, even those they're impossible to make. Most executives therefore expect to see roadmaps or plans that show how a change will take place, and they also expect to see consistent progress toward the outcome – something we talk about in a later chapter.

RESULTS MUST BE MEASURABLE AND TIED TO THE OUTCOME

One of the most difficult things we've seen when clients are facing Radical Outcomes is determining what to measure so that progress can be conveyed against the outcome, in a way that is meaningful to the executive sponsor and team at that level. Knowing that a change won't happen overnight is one important guideline, and it also implies the question: What can we measure, and in what time frame? In Maya's world, the success metric was hitting full quota for the sales roles in her division. Another metric might be a specific change in what someone is doing or demonstration of competence in a new skill, like having more conversations with your direct reports on a regular basis or using a new technology to a defined fluency.

The good thing about knowing these results? You can show the impact of what you create. You can also more readily and accurately identify gaps and make the changes needed, quickly, in an agile manner, to meet the business outcome.

Examples of business outcomes include: increased retention rates, improved acquisition rates, increased revenue, reduced costs, process improvements or efficiencies . . . increased profitability, increased word of mouth, increased conversion rates, and more upsell and cross-sell opportunities . . . they are or should all be measurable and quantifiable.[7]

Radical outcomes actually make common sense and comprise tangible results similar to what's described in the quote above. They're the product of scope and scale, and something the Executive level group is constantly envisioning. What if you could have more conversations about Radical Outcomes in your organization?

If the Outcome Isn't Clear, Ask

We've had scores of conversations with clients where they talk about an initiative they are working on with a stakeholder. Our conversation often starts with the client talking about all the stuff they believe they need to create. It's the conversation that Maya was used to having with Jack, and that shifted when Olivia asked her different types of questions. When we hear the discussion going down this path – "we need to create this stuff, that course, this presentation" – we listen, of course, and when there's a moment of pause, we tend to ask: "What's the business outcome that your stakeholder is driving toward?"

And most times, if not all times, we get a blank stare, followed by a moment of realization when our client says, "You know what, I have no idea!"

Far from being problematic, these moments are incredibly valuable for the client, because they represent the emergence of a golden opportunity for them to have a new type of conversation with their own internal customers. Suddenly there's a possibility to have a discussion that focuses on business outcomes, which can serve as a unifying construct to get different stakeholders all on the same page. Suddenly there's an opportunity to break down the silos – or, as the next chapter is about, to put divisions out of business.

Putting Divisions Out of Business

"Help me ... help you."
— from *Jerry Maguire* (TriStar Pictures, 1996)

The windowless conference room felt a bit stuffy as Olivia and a team of people sat around the table. Whiteboards filled the wall around the room, and in the middle of the table was a basket with granola bars, tangerines, and some sweet snacks. Olivia looked at her phone, and then at the clock in the room, as if to see if they matched.

"We'll see if he shows. He accepted the invite..." her voice trailed off.

"He did accept, yes," replied Jadyn.

"That's good. Better than before – he didn't even respond."

"Maybe it was the offer that we'll have snacks?" said Jadyn.

Olivia smiled. She had come to rely on Jadyn to track all of the things going on in this crazy initiative. Meetings, room setups, session notes, follow-ups for feedback, all done in a no-nonsense way that so far had worked really well to first get the stakeholder group to agree to the outcomes and measurements, and then to get people working together who might otherwise have wandered off in random directions.

Except for Marco.

Olivia looked at her watch again, wondering if he would eventually walk in the door, or if it'd be another occasion where everyone was waiting around until someone made the call to reschedule.

The door to the conference room opened, but it wasn't Marco. It was Nimit, whom Olivia had recently started working with, when the initiative was launched. Nimit was tall and lanky, and Olivia found herself wondering if he realized that he was wearing running shoes with his business casual attire. *His fashion sense hasn't seemed to matter yet*, she thought, *he still has great relationships with all of the different people on this.* In her head, she thought of all the people he'd met with, and all the lunches and coffee meetings he must have had by now. *That's like three lattes a day*, she mused.

"We have returned," he said with a smile. He entered the room with Juliana. "No Marco yet?"

Olivia shook her head and addressed Juliana. "How long should we wait this time?"

"I have a good feeling this time," Juliana answered, and at that moment the door to the conference room opened again with a knock. All heads turned to the door as Marco entered, dark-haired and wearing a colored shirt and jacket, stylish and Italian.

"Had to walk over from another building. Just so you know – I have a hard stop at 11. Hello everyone." He provided a friendly wave, and everyone shook hands politely with brief mentions of names, but when he sat down at the table his arms were folded. "Look. I'm not trying to be a jerk, but I really can't waste any time. I can't tell you how many meetings we have where I'm trying to share the information about AppSuite and the help that I need. And then . . . the stuff I get back hasn't incorporated anything that we provided. I need something that's going to help my business and the people in it."

"Totally get it, Marco," said Nimit. "I've been in those meetings, too. Here, we're using a different type of process. Just give us the next 45 minutes and have a snack."

Marco looked at the basket, and his expression softened. "Ah, pixie tangerines. I love these. Where did you get them? They are only good for a month or two out of the year. Thank you very much. So, okay. Let's get started, then?"

Olivia spoke up. "Thank you so much for giving us the time, Marco. I have a couple of questions for you, and let me just say up front that I'm not the expert in AppSuite... you are, which is why we need you for this work. I have this awesome team from Oxygen that's going to capture everything we discuss, and together we'll figure out what information is most realistic for the new hires right when they start, versus the more seasoned reps. After that, our job is to create an experience that your reps will engage with, around the content you give us."

"If you look here, the whiteboards are all set up with headlines and nothing else. By the end of this meeting we plan to fill up all the boards with the stuff from your brain. Sound good?"

"Okay, let's try it," said Marco. He put a section of the tangerine in his mouth. "Wonderful. Pixies."

Ninety minutes later, the conference room was transformed. The white boards had writing all over, and Jadyn was carefully taking pictures of each board with her phone.

"That was great, you guys!" said Olivia. She addressed Juliana. "Did you see his face light up when we showed him the whole map laid out?"

"He ate all the tangerines," said Jadyn as she framed a photo.

"You definitely have another supporter – probably your most enthusiastic one to date," said Juliana.

Nimit entered the room. "He said it was a great session, guys. We stood outside the conference room where his next meeting is, and he said he didn't want to go to it – that he'd never been in a meeting like ours, it was actually engaging and highly useful of his time." He looked at Olivia and Juliana. "Very cool. I never thought we would turn him around. He said you made it all very easy for him – that all he had to do was bring his brain! Love that. He is still wary about what's going to come next, so let's be tight."

"Thank goodness Maya intervened to get him to show up," said Olivia.

Nimit nodded. "He says this was really different from what used to happen in their group. Actually it was kind of interesting – you know what he said? 'I really just had this idea that Jack's team just didn't know what they were doing when they created stuff for us. Now that I see this way of collaborating, I'm realizing that we were a part of the problem, too. We tried to just throw an order over the fence.'" He grinned. "He said he's meeting with Garrett as well on some of the issues in that vertical. And that he'd pass along the good feedback. I'm sure it will get back to Maya."

"It's amazing what happens when you just let the expert share what they know, without trying to have all the answers as to what will happen next," said Juliana.

Nimit reflected. "Yes – the steering committee session last week was very interesting too. Lots of different perspectives, but in the end, everyone centered on the outcomes around ramp and quota. Usually those meetings go on forever and nothing gets decided concretely."

Olivia agreed, remembering back to two weeks earlier when she'd picked up the phone and called Juliana, after meeting with Jack and finding out about the initiative. Two weeks, and so much had already happened.

■ ■ ■

In May 2018, the consulting firm Deloitte published a report that shared an important trend in the way businesses are structuring themselves, from a people perspective. Rather than the traditional organization, where people tend to work in silos, and have an internal focus on their work, more and more businesses are trending toward increased collaboration, integration, and an ecosystem that focuses on customers. They call this the Social Enterprise, in which networks of teams operate in an agile way.[1] We couldn't agree more with this trend and the way that it's articulated at the macro level. However, to understand this at the micro level – that is, what the "ecosystem" means to an employee in their day-to-day job – is the reason we are writing this book!

Divisions Are Embedded in Business

In spite of the buzz about ecosystems and collaboration, people still often work as if they are divided across departments, groups, and titles. Let's face it – our brain's System 1 wants to keep things as they've always been, easily referenced, autopiloted. So it's not a surprise that Marco's expectations of how Olivia's team would engage him were set in the old way. What other evidence did he have, except to make a leap of faith (or do a favor after pressure from Maya) that things might go differently?

Our world is awash in buzzwords. The idea of collaboration has been around since humans banded together for survival, but as a concept in the world of work, it has taken off much more in the past two decades. So much so, that business leaders who are seeking to change their organizations wholesale into a more collaborative workplace have instituted sweeping measures. Which then haven't worked.

We know a CEO who desired a more collaborative workplace for his consulting business. His team responded by creating open floor plans, only to stock them full of uniform-looking cubicles and very little possibility for privacy. What was the result? Everyone brought noise-cancelling headphones to work in order to drown out the sound of phone calls and other conversations; they ducked into conference rooms for back-channel discussions; and they messaged and chatted with each other in cliques. Later, we found out that people who had been working in the same office building for *five years* had never met each other. There were major divisions in this business, and it wasn't because of the floor plan.

The problem was worse than that. Lines of business conflicted with each other. Customers complained that they were being told one thing by one division, and another thing by another division, and were getting frustrated that no one seemed to have their story straight.

Reorganizing didn't help. Introducing new products didn't help. The company continued to lose market share to their biggest competitor, who was 16 times the market cap and 10 times the revenue!

Marco is a stakeholder who came from another part of the Omen, Inc. business. What he cared about is whether the AppSuite platform that he manages is getting traction with customers. He relies on sellers to know what to do in their conversations with customers. But he's skeptical of what Jack's team has been creating for those sellers – so skeptical that he just assumed that any meetings to lay out the requirements would be a waste of his time. His business has been divided from Jack's team, both operating in their own silos. And this had to change, fast, if *anyone* – Marco, Jack, Olivia, or their audience – was going to succeed.

Where do we start, if we want to actually take the divisions out of business? One way is to start by recognizing the reality of the people around you.

Stakeholders Are People

Consider the term *stakeholder.* In our glossary, we defined a stakeholder as someone who has an interest in the outcomes and results that are being driven by the audience. In the world of work, whether we use this label or not, stakeholders matter to us because they have a role to play in the work we do and the things we set out to accomplish. They are part of those organizational groups (executives, enabling functions, audience – all serving customers) we lay out in our opening chapter, "The Why." Some might be executives. Others might be part of enabling functions. Their success is intertwined with yours, regardless of the working culture you're in. And how couldn't it be? If your company relies on many different functions to sell, service, research, develop, and market a product, aren't those teams actually all serving the customer, through your audience?

In the old way of working, your stakeholders might have been unclear about their desired outcome and tried to simply "place orders" for what they thought they needed from you. They might have responded to your work only after it was finished. This is definitely what it was like for Marco – he, or someone in his group, would say "We need more product training!" and Jack's team, rather than ask about the outcome Marco was trying to achieve, would take a look at what they had and try to update it without asking any questions. It was a lose-lose situation: as a stakeholder, Marco would just get more and more frustrated, which caused Jack's team to feel like they couldn't ask any questions, for fear of looking dumb, which then continued the vicious cycle of division. Olivia's predecessor Karina actually fell into that trap so deeply that she was paralyzed by the complexity of what was being asked, even early on in the initiative before major decisions had been made – and did nothing.

Indeed, in the old way, people on teams like Jack's tasked themselves with the bulk of the work, trying to become subject-matter experts for every project. That doesn't scale, nor does it make an impact to business outcomes. If you are doing that, you probably feel the weight of the world on your shoulders, as if you are LeBron James, but without the team.

Here are just a few things to consider that might be contributing to the gap between you and your stakeholders:

◆ Maybe stakeholders don't understand your language. Are you using unfamiliar lingo when you talk to them?

◆ Maybe subject-matter experts aren't able to contribute what they know. What kinds of questions are you asking them to draw out their ideas? (We talk more about this in Chapter 9, "Getting the Right Stuff.")

◆ Maybe it's simply hard for them to help! Ask yourself about how you can make it easier for them to engage. After all, if getting their help only complicates their world, then why would they want to engage?

Instead, what if you created an environment that makes working together so effective that your stakeholders were eager to help? What if there was willing collaboration because all understood how their goals intersected?

That sounds like a win-win to us. So how do you do that?

Here's the wonderful thing about stakeholders. They have something they need done, or a problem they need to solve, and you are going to help them. What could be more amazing?

Imagine a world where your stakeholders are vital to every stage of your work. Where they are consistently engaged and have clear context about why and how they're involved to achieve the outcome. The way we think of it, if you are simply curious about your stakeholders, their business, what they do, and how they do it, guess what happens? They give you time, their intellect, and they in turn invest in you being successful. And you become energized by their engagement.

It can be challenging at times to have this positive view. Like Marco, many stakeholders are used to seeing their input reproduced as random things. In many cases they've built a hardened shell of skepticism. So it may take a lot of message repetition, conversations, and modeling the new way before true collaboration starts to be the norm. While this new way can feel different for everyone, with upfront communication and planning, they'll realize that their contributions are valuable to the process, and they'll see where their contributions show up. They'll never want to go back to the old way, and you and they will both feel greatly unburdened. We talk even more about this in Chapter 9, "Getting The Right Stuff," where we address how to actually have these important, collaborative meetings and conversations.

Different Stakeholders, Different Conversations

One of our clients, a large telecommunications company with roughly 27,000 call-center agents, asked us to help them eliminate the random acts of training that their front-line supervisors experienced every day in the call centers. The front line supervisors who worked with the agents were a large population within this company – around 800 – and were the first escalation point for all those times when an agent would encounter something with a customer that they couldn't handle, or when hiring new agents, or making sure new product knowledge was known. They had a big impact on the business, and the people in it. And they didn't have a lot of time.

How in the heck would anyone be able to figure out what these supervisors needed from their training program, and to eliminate all the other stuff that wasn't necessary at a given point in time? Moreover, supervisors and managers tend to be the most underserved audience from an enablement standpoint, and also with the greatest need, as many supervisors must adapt to major shifts in responsibility more than most other populations in the workplace.

In the old way, this problem would have seemed like a giant boulder that had to be pushed up the hill, like the Greek fable of Sisyphus.

We took a different approach with this client. Why not dismantle that boulder into different pieces, and let our stakeholders help us help them get those pieces up the hill? Here are three things you can do to change the way you talk with stakeholders and take the divisions out of your business.

- ◆ Engage your stakeholders, by asking questions and being curious.
- ◆ Give them a specific role on the project, by recognizing what they are responsible for in the business, and how that can be additive to the outcome.
- ◆ Make it easy for them to participate, by having empathy for their time constraints, and design working sessions with clear, manageable objectives.

ENGAGING YOUR STAKEHOLDERS

We've written this entire book to formulate a new way of working that can be used to drive toward Radical Outcomes. Let's remember, though, that your stakeholders may not have read this book (though we hope they will)! With that in mind, rather than attempting to "sell them" on a new way of doing things, try to model the way for them. In fact, if you dwell on the idea of a new process right up front, you might not get a very favorable response. If you think about it, most of your stakeholders care less about what your process is, and more about the outcome. So, however you have to get there, that's what works for them. Spend the time you have to focus in on what's needed from them, how you will work together, and setting expectations as clearly and specifically as possible. Don't get us wrong: we love process, but your stakeholders love getting their outcome, so stay focused on that when you talk to them.

How exactly do you go out and engage people in the business that you support? If salespeople are your audience, ask to go on some sales calls with reps. If you support leaders, ask if you can sit in on some of their team meetings, have lunch with their people, be curious, and ask questions. Like Nimit in our story, whose ability to connect with stakeholders far outpaced his fashion sense, work toward empathy for what's involved in their job. Later, when it comes time to determine what is going to be helpful or a burden for your audience, you'll want to channel your stakeholders' knowledge, and use that to decide what needs to be created.

You might have gathered that, in spite of Nimit's odd dress code, he was skilled at building his network and relationships. The more you build your own understanding of how different parts of the business operate, the more it will help you in your career. Building business relationships is twofold: it's interpersonal, and it's business related. If you are able to expand your knowledge and business relationships, you'll become more and more valuable in the role that you play.

This might seem basic, but we find that it's very overlooked. We have often seen instead that people tend to be more concerned with showing their expertise, even when the areas of expertise needed for the outcome are so broad and deep, that no one human could possibly know it all!

To engage your stakeholders, we've learned that taking the time to have empathy for other enabling functions and areas of the business is far more valuable than showing what kind of expertise you have. While expertise is also important, it's about a balance between having a point of view about a subject, and getting so steeped in that subject that it can't be easily described to others. We talk more about this in Chapter 9, "Getting The Right Stuff."

GIVING YOUR STAKEHOLDERS A ROLE

To dismantle that Sisyphean boulder, stakeholders need context on what is potentially expected of them as you work together toward the outcome. What kind of role do they play? It depends on what their role is, in the business.

Figure 6.1 shows some of those roles, and ways to position their role on the team.

- ◆ **Executive Sponsor.** The executive sponsor is a business group leader, similar to the role that Maya has in Omen, Inc. The executive sponsor will have a business metric attached to the audience being successful – such as reducing time to quota and staying in role longer.

    How to talk to them: Tell us what specific outcomes you are driving. How will those outcomes drive the business goals?

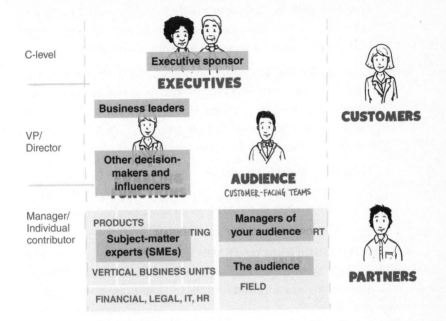

FIGURE 6.1 Your Stakeholders

- ◆ **Business Leaders.** Often times, leaders from across the lines of business contribute to initiatives by participating on a steering committee. Their role is to provide both a strategic view for the audience, as well as a representation of the realities that audience faces every day. Garrett, Maya's peer, is in a role similar to hers and experiences the same angst about his sellers being unprepared to have the right conversations with customers.

  How to talk to them: Explain to us the challenges that you see your sellers facing or that you are reporting on that could be better. Also, who are strong performers in your organization whom we could talk to?

- ◆ **The Audience.** In order to really understand your audience, you'll need to speak with people who have had success in their role. This kind of invaluable input can later help to establish a structure (architecture) for what works in the business environments they face.

How to talk to them: Since I don't do your job, I need your help to understand your world, so that I can serve you by providing a relevant learning experience.

◆ **Managers of Your Audience.** It helps to have the people who manage your audience involved so that you can get buy-in and a different lens on their realities. Buy-in is important! If they get engaged and support what is being created, they have critical influence over ensuring their people use it.

How to talk to them: We need your help so that we can help you – if we provide simple, easy, conversation guidelines for you to connect with your team as they go through this shift, would that be helpful?

◆ **Subject-Matter Experts (SMEs).** These are the people who, like Marco, have tons of information in their head – but they often need the most help to get that knowledge to scale across the audience!

How to talk to them: You know a lot. Way more than we do. We can't do it without your knowledge. Please help us help you by working together to distill the top three things the audience must know and do to be successful when they first start.

◆ **Other Decision-makers and Influencers.** Sometimes there are others who want to be involved or have influence. It's good to remember these people and include them strategically and as needed, to have more influence. They can be at different levels of the organization, not just at the executive level.

How to talk to them: This is what we are creating and why. I would love to hear what you think about it and how to ensure its success.

What happens with all this engagement? It needs to be orchestrated and distilled into something that will help your audience be successful in their role. Imagine if, instead of simply facilitating the knowledge, you approached this task by assuming you needed to be an expert in each of these stakeholder realms. In our view, that boulder would still be at the bottom of the hill even today.

MAKE IT EASY FOR YOUR STAKEHOLDERS

In Olivia's meeting, Marco was clearly delighted by the pixie tangerines. To that end, we always advocate having snacks when a hard-working, face-to-face meeting is to take place. What's behind that idea, though?

As we learn in a more colorful chapter about how to run sessions with stakeholders, if you spend some time really making the engagement feel lightweight for them, it will actually be easier for everyone to assimilate information and get on the same page. We like to say to people: "We're going to have a conversation. We'll take all the notes, document everything, and summarize it. All you have to do is bring your brain!"

We like to think of it as unburdening our stakeholders. For example, what if you invite busy stakeholders who haven't eaten lunch before your session? A mix of snacks helps them get some fuel and they'll be grateful for it. Sometimes it's the little things that ensure that the energy in the session is maintained positively.

As stakeholders realize that their contributions are valuable to the process and are applied, you and they will both feel greatly unburdened. This alone can be incredibly powerful. And again, reaching this point can take quite a bit of message repetition, conversations, and modeling in the new way.

We've found that if we are curious, open and make it easy to engage, then others will follow suit. In Olivia's meetings, she had a new stakeholder enter a meeting not knowing anything about the process beyond what was in their email invite, filled with skepticism about our promised turnaround times and willingness to incorporate feedback. She stuck to commitments and showed them progress that included their input and made the process of meetings fun and collaborative, and what happened? Marco became an advocate.

One Simple Idea: We Are All Human

No matter what stakeholders you work with, there's one common tenet that is simple but goes a long way: stakeholders are people, and people like to engage with authenticity.

We can expect that the results from people are commensurate with the way they are treated. People who treat others as if they need to recognize credentials first, or begin by giving orders, or who constantly provide platitudes to cover for their insecurities, aren't going to be successful in getting others to work in a collaborative way. In fact, they'll more likely to start reverting to protective behavior, like back channeling, wearing headphones to tune out the noise, and avoiding other people in the same building.

Additionally, with all of the complexity in today's world of work, let's face it: simple answers to complex problems don't simply arise from the mind of one person. So why pretend or posture as if we have those answers? Instead, let's just let reality be what it is, and recognize that even if we don't have the answer now, we can get there through collaborating and assuming that people will bring the best of themselves to the table. In this way, people can relax, and they don't have to anticipate the answer. And the results that happen when people work this way are amazing.

ENVIRONMENT

The Experience Is Human

The only source of knowledge is experience.
—Albert Einstein, theoretical physicist

The train was packed and humid as the overcrowded car crawled over the bridge. Raindrops showed up as diagonal lines on the window, where a foggy skyline provided a backdrop to traffic and taillights lined up next to the train tracks. *At least we're going slightly faster than they are*, Olivia thought as they passed a blue Mustang at a cyclists' pace. She looked out the window and then checked her phone. *Hopefully there'll still be time, at this late juncture, to pick up morning coffee...*

The train halted and was overtaken by the Mustang... *Or maybe not.*

Resigned, she turned her mind back to work.

A week and a half earlier, the commute had gone without a hitch as Olivia headed in to the office. On that day, there had been plenty of time to open the app on her phone and place her usual order at Coffee Place at One Technology Plaza, right on the corner where the station emerges onto the street, just a block from the Omen, Inc., office. Three minutes after placing the order on the app, she would exit the train, walk briskly up the stairs, head out onto street level, through the rotating doors of One Technology Plaza, and pick up her soy cappuccino and turkey bacon and egg sandwich from the stand.

83

On that day of the smooth commute, she'd swept in to pick up her order, and without stopping, pivoted away from the counter just as a man, also clearly in a hurry, walked straight into her coffee.

"Nooo!" they both said, as the full coffee cup fell onto the counter.

"Whoa," said the barista as beige liquid splashed the surface.

"I'm so sorry," said the man, "Did you get any on you? Jeez."

Olivia checked her shirt. "I think I'm okay," as others crowded nearby to pick up their orders. She looked up at the counter where her coffee had spilled, and the barista had already mopped up most of the damage.

"Shelley's making another one for you right now," said the barista.

"I gotta run," said the man. "Really sorry..."

Olivia had stepped back, and back further still, to allow the commuters to shimmy up to the counter. She looked at how the crowd movement never stopped – any one person who came through to pick up their mobile order was only there for 30 seconds, then gone. She watched the baristas and staff as they talked to one another, handed off, reached around each other, called out customer names.

What an amazing system, she thought.

"Soy cappuccino for Olivia!" Olivia looked at the counter, which two minutes earlier had been the site of a chaotic coffee spill. She picked up her coffee and, instead of briskly walking out the other side of the café, continued watching the scene, transfixed, her focus moving across the café as she looked at the people, the bustle, the displays.

It's the experience, she'd thought then. *Oh, my gosh. We've been thinking about it all wrong...*

The train lurched, then stopped. Olivia was jolted out of her thoughts about the day of the coffee spill. The blue Mustang was nowhere to be seen. "Apologies for the delay, disabled train in front of us," croaked a barely audible announcement. Olivia and others around her groaned. She flipped apps on her phone and dialed a number.

"Hey, it's me," she said. "Train issues. Can you start without me? I think I'm going to be about 15 minutes late. I'll need you to walk through the beginning part – to set the context." She paused, looking around to make sure she wasn't talking too loudly. "It should be in the first couple of slides. It's the whole thing where Maya is asking for "world-class results," but someone has to ask the question, what the heck does that mean? And then pivot them toward how it's about their role and their experience that is the real design point."

She smiled. "Just make one of your jokes where you confuse what you are supposed to wear between cricket and tennis," she said. "Oh, and seriously – that slide where it calls out how we attended sales calls – that is super important, if you get to that point before I arrive. Like that one for United Bank? Where there were like 19 of our people at the meeting? So the talk track for that is...think about the complexity that an account manager has to deal with, just in orchestrating all of our teams in such a huge account and large deal. You should tell them about the part where five of them had never met each other before, and the account manager had to remind them not to do first-meeting small talk in front of the client..."

The train lurched again, moved several feet, then stopped. "Jeez. I might be later than 15 minutes, Nimit," she said. "So, on that same slide, remember to talk about how we listened in on the internal planning calls, to ask questions about how they work. That one photo – that's Barry Rothenberg, remember he sent that to us showing the remote office? He was like, 'I don't care how it looks, just make sure it's useful to me, and that I can get it on my phone, otherwise I just won't use it.'

"Yes, make sure you look at the interview transcript for Barry. He's the one who received 50 emails of required training from his training group. Fifty individual required trainings. Fifty." Olivia made a face palm while talking. "How much time does that add up to? He didn't know how to prioritize what was sent to him, he assumed it wasn't all relevant, he didn't have the time to spend to do it all, so then what happened. He just didn't do any of it! He just went online and searched for stuff he thought he needed. Jeez...what a waste..."

Olivia paused and looked out the window. "We have to show the committee what it's like to be in the sellers' shoes, Nimit. So they can understand why we're doing it this way. You know...going slow to move fast...just trying to make this useful for their people. Whoa!" The train lurched and moved, this time continuing to pick up speed. "Okay, we're moving. See you in a bit," she said, and hung up.

• • •

We are living in an age of experience. The explosive growth of the information age has given way to the empowered customer, where options, choices, and ways to spend money have become so multi-faceted that companies have recognized that the only way to retain customers is to delight them by offering unique experiences. When Olivia breezes through Coffee Place without having to stop (unless someone runs into her), it's already a foregone conclusion that, as long as that experience is consistent, she'll continue to spend money almost every day at that café. And not only that, but Olivia will seek out that same experience when traveling and in other parts of the world, anticipating the same easy routine that has become a norm.

Think about the sheer number of variables involved in making Olivia's morning commute, including its Coffee Place stop, go smoothly. The timing of the train; the weather; the operation of the assembly line; the number of other customers ordering; the stuff on the menu; the availability of ingredients . . . we could make a list as long as this book about the vast amount of stuff that is being orchestrated to make that experience go as well as it has for Olivia.

What if Olivia, as the customer, had to factor in all of that complexity? Chances are, she'd eat breakfast at home and Coffee Place would not have the opportunity to serve her or have her willingly part ways with the $9.45 that could arguably be spent elsewhere.

But Coffee Place was able to consider all those variables and make deliberate decisions about how to structure the experience so that it would be easy for Olivia. That also included knowing which of those variables would be out of their control and up to her to decide (such as the train timing, or the weather). It also meant figuring out what items in the flow would be most critical to the timing of her experience. It meant lots of coordination between the technology components of her experience and then the human things that happen in the moment at that store.

We Can All Relate to Good Experiences – And Bad

As consumers, we can relate to Olivia's experience, as well as many others that have been created for us. Netflix changed the way that people received DVDs, by making the choosing and receiving of the DVD a very simple experience. Everything had been thought through: all done online, delivered to your home with a packet ready for you to send it back in, with no more late fees or running to the store to grab a movie on Friday night, only to find it's no longer available. Then, as DVDs quickly became obsolete, Netflix adapted, and continued offering consumers an effortless experience through content streaming and creation.

In the hospitality sector, Airbnb evolved from crowd-sourced lodging to enabling people to literally choose the type of experience they want to have, from concerts to cooking to social impact. Consumer-facing businesses have reinvented themselves to deliver experiences first, products and services second.

Indeed, poor customer experience has led to the death of some industries, like the traditional taxi industry. You've probably felt the frustration of calling a dispatch and then hoping to get a cab, the unpredictable cleanliness (or lack thereof) of those cabs, and then feeling obliged to tip and never knowing the right amount. In response to suboptimal experiences like this, Uber arrived and disrupted that market, fast. In fact, most of the apps on your phone have used disruption of industry and market as a design principle – from ordering books to finding cheap flights to tracking exercise to gaming. What makes it possible? The experience. But not just any experience.

Customer Experience Is a Thing

What does a customer experience mean? In a nutshell, it boils down to this:

- ◆ The experience delivers value to customers.
- ◆ It's easy to get value from the experience.
- ◆ Customers feel good about their experience and come back repeatedly for it.

What we haven't seen – and why we are writing this book – is the question of *how* to create the experiences that help people achieve radical outcomes, and what *good* actually looks like when it comes to that nitpicky fact that people are humans, living in a complex, digital world.

Why Aren't People Able to Learn at Work?

Let's think about what probably happens when Olivia arrives at her office building on that rainy day. All those sources of stress we share in earlier chapters about the complexity in the workplace: the information overload, the random tasks we encounter and try to manage, the stress of having too much on one's plate, and the unsettling amount of time and money wasted on trying to help people do things differently at work, but not moving the needle. For a lot of people, this is the reality inside the office.

It is a world of work that delivers a suboptimal experience. Or perhaps more accurately, it's a world of work in which existing structures conflict with each other. Some structures that might have worked in the past aren't adjusted to meet business outcomes that have changed; others might be new, executive-level directives where the work hasn't been done within the enabling functions to figure out how to help people to be successful.

Imagine what would happen if Coffee Place promised an app with mobile ordering, that Olivia downloaded it with the expectation of ordering, and that every time she hit the *order* button, the app crashed, her card was charged, and she kept ending up with a tall drip coffee, black, instead of a venti soy latte. The expectation of mobile ordering was set, but the experience routinely failed.

The same is often true for many people working today. Just like in Chapter 6, "Putting Divisions Out of Business," where the CEO tries to encourage collaboration with the open floor plan, there's a lot more to an experience than just office layout. As it turned out, this company had over a dozen locations in different time zones that required its consultants to be on the phone with each other for many hours a day. People were accustomed to scheduling lots of back-to-back phone calls, which made it difficult to book conference rooms, let alone travel between them; it was easier to stay at one's desk. The nature of the conversations was often argumentative – positively so, but there was a lot of stuff that these consultants had to figure out together, so it was hard for people to concentrate if they had to overhear such conversations. The big miss with the so-called "collaborative" floor plan: no one had attempted to find out what type of work people did, and whether the open plan would be conducive to that type of work.

TODAY'S WORK EXPERIENCE IS MISSING THE MARK

We are certain that you have had a first-hand encounter with a suboptimal work experience. Who hasn't? Think about a time when you first joined a company in a new role and went through some sort of onboarding – if any was offered at all. In our interviews with all kinds of customer-facing individuals such as customer service agents, account managers, even the managers of salespeople – they told us that their onboarding consisted of lots of details about benefits and filling out paperwork. Others said they spent two weeks or more feeling as if they were drinking from a fire hose of information. One interviewee told us, "My onboarding was basically nothing at all, just being handed a computer and told 'good luck!'"

Throughout the interviews, the language we kept hearing to describe onboarding was about information overload, or being left on one's own to figure it all out. And yet, as we've mentioned, businesses spend over \$140 billion per year on training, learning technology, and development.[1]

In the midst of all the interruption, information, and constant churn of fire drills, tasks, and priorities, all of us – whether we are leaders, individual contributors, or specialists, whether we work with customers or support those who do – are part of the same urgent directive to learn and adapt as quickly as possible to our shifting businesses. But how?

A lot of the information overload – the phenomenon inside workplaces that can overwhelm and bog down the brain to the point that we've dubbed it "noise" – is made up of stuff that is not critical. It's nice to have. It won't have direct impact to the point of creating newfound or ongoing success. Consider it a garnish for the cocktail of tasks and responsibilities we take on every day.

In the environment we live in, no one has time for nice-to-have. If a tool or a platform doesn't clearly demonstrate how it'll help us work, we're wasting time trying to implement it into our daily rhythms. There needs to be a better way to focus on what's imperative to success.

MEETING THE AUDIENCE WHERE THEY'RE AT

What's really going on when people have a suboptimal learning experience at work? When an investment is made to create something for them to learn, or change, or acquire a new skill, or have a different kind of conversation with a customer – why is it that, after that person has gone through the training experience, nothing changes?

Here is what we have found: *suboptimal learning experiences fail to meet the audience where they're at.*

Another way to say this is: if you don't know your audience, and where they stand in their journey at work, how can you ensure that they have a good experience in consuming what you create for them? And how do we define a good experience – for them?

Think of all the examples we've raised about information overload. It's almost as if the people creating all that stuff, or just sending over whatever they had, forgot altogether that on the receiving end of that stuff are humans! A recent LinkedIn report found that "Less than 1/4 of L&D professionals surveyed are willing to recommend their own L&D programs to peers."[2] The B2C companies we mentioned earlier, and many others, have managed to crack the code on great experiences for their customers. *It was valuable. It was easy. It felt like it was made for me.* Why must it be worse at work?

This is what's missing when people are tasked to learn and asked to do more: the experiences created for them simply don't have them in mind. Taking time out of a busy day to learn a new tool, attend a workshop, or share progress at a team meeting are all activities that end up with negative associations. *The experience of participating feels worthless. Sitting through it is hard. I use the time to do other things.*

One of the first questions that we tend to ask our clients is, "Who is the audience that you're serving?" Aside from broad terms such as "salespeople," "technical sellers," "front line managers," we find that most people don't actually know their audience. They make assumptions, or their perception is based on what a small group of people thinks, or their perspective is outdated or associated only to the job description.

One client we worked with needed to up-skill their call-center agents, so a team created a virtual classroom course to be delivered online, only to realize that not all of the call centers had computers with video cards. Imagine how the agents felt about that experience, and what they missed in learning to be successful in their role, because they couldn't consume what was created for them. Imagine the cost that was sunk into this course, which had to be redesigned, and all of the consequences of loss of time and funds. On the receiving end of random acts, agents received mandatory notice to take a course, clicked on it, and realized they couldn't complete it.

Think about that. You've been told to do something because it's essential for your success at work, but no one seems to know that you won't have the technology necessary to complete this task.

These misses – which happen across industries with alarming frequency and cost – can be avoided if you take the approach that the experiences created for your audience need to recognize the humans in the audience that are being served. If you start thinking about what is most helpful for you at work, and are curious and ask others around you, you'll start to build that empathy.

Human Objectives Create a Human Experience

What can you do to create a good experience, when so much has shifted around what "good" looks like? If you're working backwards from Radical Outcomes, Good means "How relevant, easy, accessible and engaging is the thing that we create?" And this means, *start with knowing your audience.*

We have found that knowing three simple, human aspects about your audience can help immensely in creating something that truly meets your audience where they're at.

Audience Realities. What kind of environment does your audience work in? How do they get information, both at work and out of work? Knowing what they do on the job as they seek out what they need to know is great – and, knowing what they do when they're not on the clock tells you what they do with their own time, and how you can make their work learning more similar to their everyday learning. What constraints do they have? Are they remote workers? Do they spend a lot of time in a car or out at meetings? Do they have an office or do they work in an open-plan cubicle? Are they paid by the hour or salaried? What does their typical workweek look like? Where do they go regularly at work to find information that they might need?

Asking these types of questions will help you start to figure out the experience that is going to make the biggest impact on your audience. By understanding their circumstances, you can then create something that is going to fit into their workday easily, be easy to consume, so that they can keep progressing in their day-to-day responsibilities, and after the experience they are much better off.

Audience Role. Knowing the role of your audience is critical. And yet we see many assumptions made about people's roles without really understanding the details. What is the person's job and how is it changing? Are you sure you're clear about whether there are multiple roles in your consideration? A front-line supervisor's world, where they help agents with phone calls or customer escalations, is probably quite different from the job of the manager of the call-center group, where they orchestrate resources and work on scheduling and reporting. If you create the same experience for both audiences, then the material may not be relevant to *either*. Additionally, any person brings their prior knowledge to their job and role, and this needs to be factored in. Are they seasoned sellers who are new to a particular role? Or are they young adults hired to make high volumes of phone calls? For each of these audiences, what they need to know and do is not the same.

Time Frame of the Role. One of the major misses that we see in terms of understanding an audience is the reality that a human being learns over time, not all at once, and certainly not at a single event. What is reasonable to expect from someone who is new to their role? How much will they be able to do in the first 90 days? What if you are helping a group of experienced engineers to integrate a new product, and most of the team has been with the company for five years or more? These scenarios are different, and need to be factored in if the experience you are creating is to be relevant. This can seem like a "duh" statement, yet across all of the clients that we have worked with, they consistently overlook the fact that when it comes to how people learn, one can process only so much information – just as we articulate in Chapter 1, "The Why." When working with subject-matter experts, we often repeat this point: "We're at day 45 in this person's role. Do they *really* need this amount of information at day 45?" By constantly referring to a time frame, we were able to extract a more realistic and digestible breakdown of the content that is second nature to a SME.

> The onboarding process is always the tough part. In sales, the goal is to get you ramped up as fast as possible. [But] the experience is usually like drinking from a fire hose. It's too much information, too fast, and frankly, most of the information is stuff that you wouldn't even need until you've been on the job for six months. You're given it in the first six weeks and you will have forgotten most of it by the time you got there.
>
> —Dave L., Sales Manager[3]

When these human objectives are used to create an experience at work, the result feels different to your audience, as shown in Figure 7.1. And when it works, you'll find that the audience will develop similar loyalties to their role and their job, just as Olivia returns to Coffee Place each day.

I am taken care of   I am thinking for myself

I am able to use technology – and it's easy

I am able to practice

I have a safe way to make mistakes

I didn't even realize I was learning!

I am confident enough to use what I learned in real life

FIGURE 7.1   How a Good Experience Lands with Your Audience

But hang on. We may have just made this all sound easy, as if we might be overlooking the complexity in your environment There's still a lot of information that people need to know! There are still so many random requests! How does knowing the audience help with all of that information, and how do we prioritize the thousand things that our stakeholders say that people "should" do?

The answer to that question is covered in the next chapter, about architecture.

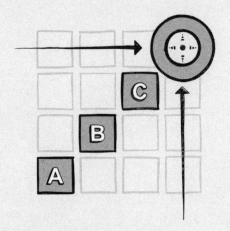

ARCHITECT

Why We Can't Live without Architecture

You cannot defend your design without knowing what you're designing for.

—I.M. Pei

"Okay, Marvin. Thanks for the updates – we'll review the work in more detail and keep you posted," said Olivia as Marvin gathered his laptop and papers, and exited the conference room.

"Nice to meet you all," he said to everyone. "Thanks, Olivia." All eyes watched the door shut behind him.

Olivia turned around back to the group, her eyes wide and stunned. She put both her hands to her face and her elbows on the table, among the printed pages of a spreadsheet with many rows and columns.

"Oh ... mrrrr ... gssff," her muffled voice came through her hands. She pulled her hands away, straightened up, and faced the group. "What do we do about this?"

Juliana nodded. "Yes. That was a lot of stuff."

Olivia grabbed a page of the printout. "Three hundred? How are we supposed to verify what he said? How can 300 online ... *thingies* ... all be important?" She stood up and started pacing. "This is what I mean. Nobody is thinking about how it all adds up. What new hire is going to take the time to go through 300 things in their first month on the job? They have to start actually talking to customers! And that was just the stuff from Marvin, from our team. Every single business group in this initiative has been sending me product knowledge requirements, capabilities – things the new hires have to be able to talk about..."

Olivia kept on talking. "None of it is connected! It's all just lists of topics. Who's supposed to decide what's actually important? How do we validate that?" She paused. "Okay... now I'm just repeating what I said to him... sorry, you were saying?"

"No worries. Yes. Agreed," said Juliana, "Without any documentation as to what's in each item in his list, or who's actually been through it, or if it's been updated... you're basically blind."

"I mean," Olivia said, getting agitated again, "There is no way of knowing whether updates have been made."

"Or whether additional components are available such as on-the-job activities, job aides, or links to other materials," said Juliana, "let alone what the actual content consists of. Is the stuff in the courses right for someone that was in their first 120 days on the job? Is it too deep to make sense to someone new?"

"Right. And based on all the other stuff I'm getting, there could be competing models being used for different concepts," said Olivia. "And there's all this stuff from different third-party vendors where we bought the IP or licensed it."

"And there's no consistent messaging, branding, or logic for the intended audiences," said Juliana.

Olivia buried her face in her hands again.

"Look," said Juliana. "This kind of randomness and overload is not surprising. Think of how much change has happened in your industry. It's no wonder there's no global onboarding program and no consistency. It's not that people are doing a bad job. They just don't have a way to organize all the complexity."

Olivia looked at all the printouts on the table. "So much complexity," she said. "And I've looked at this stuff. It's so outdated. Why even use it at all?"

"One thing is really clear, Olivia," said Juliana. "Rivers wants to be able to shorten the sellers' ramp-up time, and also have a consistent experience globally. And Maya has also made it clear after hearing so much from the field that the content for these sellers is really bad. Which means: we probably need to replace it."

"So much stuff," said Olivia. "I can't believe this is what we do to our people – to overload them. Those sales meetings that I went to, to see what their world is like...there is no way they have time to consume all this."

"You're right. No human being can. It's too much."

"Guys – what do we do here?"

Juliana turned to face Katherine, who had been sitting at the end of the table, watching the conversation and occasionally sketching on blank pieces of paper.

"This is what we do," Katherine said. "We create an architecture."

Olivia blinked. *A what? For this?* "How..." she started.

Katherine went to the whiteboard. "So..." her voice trailed off as she drew a series of long rectangles across the top.

Juliana looked at Olivia. "Katherine is doing her thing, you know," she said, smiling.

"Look," said Katherine, drawing. "We know the business outcome. Shorten sellers' ramp-up time. That's something we can actually measure. Right?"

"And we know their roles – that stuff is really well documented," said Juliana. "Thank goodness. Or we'd have to run that to ground."

"So then," said Katherine, writing and talking, "We create a structure that allows us to sequence stuff – all that stuff, what is it? It's *what* they need to know and do? *When* do they need to know and do it? In their first 120 days. You've got your boundaries right there. Sorry, my lefty handwriting is terrible – can you read that?"

Juliana picked up a marker. "Exactly – and we draft it, and will map stuff in here, we'll take a best guess based on what you know, Olivia, but it's not the whole answer. It's enough for you to have the conversation, though, and ask, does someone *really* need to know and do this thing or that thing in their first 120 days? What's the minimum, the one thing..."

Olivia stood up and looked at the white board. "Oh, wow. Wow. So like, you have this high level thing you want them to achieve, over here, that connects to ramp-up – what's ramp up? They'll say it's quota. We can validate that. So maybe the first thing to that would be, get familiar with Omen, Inc. It's like...I was just reading about this," Olivia flipped to a page in her notebook. "'An important task or duty that is assigned, allotted, or self-imposed' – it's a *mission!*"

"Yes! And...you know you've achieved the mission when, say, you can do a roleplay with someone who really knows the business," said Juliana.

"Right, right. Then what would go into that? How do we break that all up?"

"How about it's like an episode?" said Juliana. "After all, we want all of this to be binge-worthy."

"Yes! And so we could sequence it...maybe include...this online material?"

"Yes, and at the same time you'll want to break that up with some other activities. You don't want them to have to be at a screen for more than 15 minutes, right?"

"Right! Okay. So there's that manager council that's developed a mentor program. We could tap in to that..."

"And, they could also just go have a conversation with a peer, as part of the flow. But about this specific topic on getting to know the customer. Which is what the business owners said was so important. So when you reflect that here, they'll see that their input was factored in."

"Oh, right. And you could check that the seller did that...by asking the manager to validate..."

After several hours, the papers on the table were organized into piles, and the whiteboard – which ran the length of the room – was filled with a sequence of rectangles and writing underneath. The group stepped back and looked around the room.

"Wow. There's so much stuff that didn't make it in," said Olivia.

"We're going to have to rebuild it all," said Olivia.

"Yes, I think so," Juliana nodded.

"It's got to be flexible. We have to be able to change it as the business changes. Like software releases!"

"If they can do it with your phone apps, why not this?" said Juliana.

"But now with all of this laid out, it'll be easy to maintain."

Juliana nodded. "Yes. You'll be able to easily locate exactly the content that needs changing. And you'll be able to discuss with the stakeholders as to why something doesn't fit."

"We need to make sure we measure the results of the sellers who go through this," said Olivia.

"We can do all of that. Because...guess what we just did," said Katherine. "We created an architecture."

■　■　■

Consider a moment when you entered a building or a structure and felt compelled to notice your place within its structure. The building could have been a museum, the foyer of a skyscraper, or something much simpler – your house, a dorm room or first apartment. The structure could have been the waiting area of a major train station, or the cool car that you sat in while visiting the showroom just to see what it was like.

That we are able to have some kind of experience upon entering a space or structure, and able to comprehend with our eyes and senses that the space was built for a purpose with us in mind, is the core idea of why architecture exists. Every little buzz of your senses, whether it's the way light cascades in through windows regardless of the sun's angle in the sky, or the magnificent expansiveness of high ceilings, or the sheer ability to accommodate thousands of humans in one place – all of this had to be considered and built for a purpose.

Moreover, that purpose extends beyond our experience in the moment. It encompasses the structure's sustainability amid changing conditions, or its adaptability to different uses – a football game on one day, an arena for a rock concert on another.

We also know very well what it feels like to experience bad architecture. The parking garage that creates its own traffic jams due to poor design of lanes, spaces, and turns. The sagging back porch that can't be used for fear of collapse. The kitchen whose layout puts the dishwasher in one corner and the sink in another. Bad architecture is inconvenient, annoying, and can even be dangerous. It represents wasteful or inconsiderate use of available resources. It's ugly and mostly becomes unusable at some point, or a constant drag to use.

All of the aspects of architecture we've described above are easy to imagine because we've experienced them in tangible space, within physical structures that we can touch and feel. To take that physical perspective, architecture is an assembly of material elements intended for human inhabitation and use.

Think about Chapter 7, "The Experience Is Human," in which Olivia breezes through the Coffee Place line to get her coffee.

This kind of experience merges technology with fulfillment in a seamless way, and is something that we've all come to expect in the modern, connected world. It's amazing and yet we use it without much marveling. Only when it doesn't work do we grumble about the inconvenience. But most of the time, it works flawlessly, like magic.

It isn't magic. It's architecture.

Imagine that Coffee Place is developing their mobile ordering experience. Before all the employees did the actual work to create the app that enables the experience, they needed an architecture to describe the work that would be done to create and deliver it. Different pieces of the project needed to fit together just so, so that the app itself worked as intended. And when parts of the app failed, some of those same developers needed that architecture in order to easily find the problem and service that portion of the code.

Olivia's team created their own architecture, to enable the experience they envisioned for their audience, and also for the ability to easily maintain and update it. All the things they wanted the audience to be able to know and do were sequenced into Missions and Episodes, so that the experience would *feel* right to them. And creating the architecture enabled the flexibility and adaptability to change. Figure 8.1 shows the attributes that go into a good experience, and how architecture enables those attributes.

At the end of the day, audiences don't need to care about any of these behind-the-scenes structures. Coffee Place architected Olivia's experience so that she could decide when to time her order. And they came up with contingencies for when things don't go right – like quickly remaking her coffee after it was spilled on the counter. She got rewards for ordering using the app, and a free coffee every once in a while. For the customer, it just feels easy. They'll keep going back, as long as it stays that way – and they'll seek out those brands that make it easy wherever they go. Amazing.

Architecture Ain't Your Enemy – It's Your Friend

How do you react to the word architecture? You might be relieved that someone is finally talking about it in a book like this. Or, as

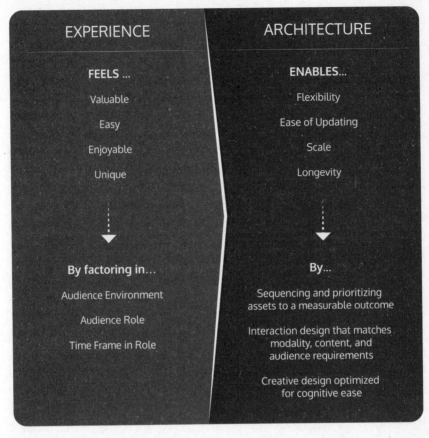

FIGURE **8.1**   Experience Feels Like Something, Architecture Enables It

we've experienced when talking to clients and colleagues, architecture might sound too complicated, like an extra project that you'd never have time to actually tackle.

We asked around our networks for different definitions of architecture and looked for ones that didn't necessarily pertain to physical structures. Here's what we got:

The framework or structure of something.

—A graphic designer

Architecture is about serving others through the design of the built environment.

—Kevin J. Singh[1]

Architecture is the total system, consisting of subordinate systems and structures, plus how they fit together. Too often, these architectures come with rules that allow it to grow but without rules to change, or that drive maladaptive processes into extinction. In this rigidity, everything persists too long, even those things that shouldn't. Organizational health requires both growth and extinction processes.

—Kenneth P. Pitts[2]

Structure. Serving others through design. The total system, and how things fit together. These all sound like welcome additions in a world of work that is overloaded with noise and random stuff. So when it comes to what we create for other people so that they can use it, to do their work more effectively, and be more successful at work, why does the perception persist that embracing structure will slow everything down?

Our view is that it's hard for people to let go of what they know, even if it will help. Remember Kahneman's System 1?[3] It's great in a pinch, when you need to talk and drive at the same time, or immediately flee for your survival from a burning building. But it also gets in the way of the consideration needed to shift what we do in the face of other, less dire changes. The changes that we experience at work are not going to kill us at a given moment; they are larger shifts whose effects we don't immediately feel. For example, when it's announced that your company is going to merge with another company, does that change your day-to-day job at the moment you receive the news? Probably not. In light of the non-dire nature of that change, it probably seems okay to most people to just do what they've always done. In effect, this is allowing System 1 to keep calling the shots, *even if this approach will slowly undermine the system we are part of.*

That slow undermining starts to weigh on everyone, to the point where you accept it as table stakes that having a job means constant pressure to do more, produce more, work more hours, take fewer breaks. We already know that this kind of hyperloaded environment takes a major toll on people and their ability to be productive, as Dan Pink elaborates in his recent book, *When: The Scientific Secrets of Perfect Timing.*[4]

But it's hard to break those habits, especially in the absence of an alternative.

We Can Choose to Use Architecture – Or Just Do the Same Old Thing

It's common to believe that there isn't enough time for architecture. It's true creating an architecture can feel slow or heavy, and that because of the pace and the pressure people are under, they might feel constant pressure to be creating something, anything, to show value to the organization.

In the meeting room where Olivia put her head in her hands after Marvin left, we saw the many random things (300 online thingies, to be exact) that become part of programs that lack architecture. Or rather, whatever structure might have existed before, and might have been useful, cannot stand up to the complexities of today's working environment. In that room, Olivia and her team were faced with some costly options: either go through and catalog all of the old things, with a fair amount of certainty that after cataloguing, much would still have to be replaced; or make the call that the material was outdated, too long, and too expensive to modify, in both content and modality. Without knowing if the material was even going to help someone new to their sales role, Olivia realized she was going to have to scrap it all and start over.

She knew this audience had to have easily consumable, job-relevant, actionable training materials during onboarding.

She knew that whatever she built, it needed to stand the test of time and be easy to update as content needs shifted. Her team would need to be able to easily identify outcomes and the pieces of content that drive them – and then when the outcomes shift, to locate the piece of the experience that needs to change to stay relevant to the sellers' success.

By building an architecture up front, we can be much more certain that we aren't perpetrating more random acts or creating something that isn't usable. We can design any output, any process, any experience, so that it can be changed easily because it's documented all along the way. The structure, planning, and architecture makes the execution happen rapidly.

Just as with the architecture of physical things like buildings or bridges, nothing built at work lasts through time without thinking carefully about the structure. The amount of time required for that up-front planning depends on the complexity of the endeavor; and we have found that, no matter how big or small, if we take the time to work on the architectural aspects of a project, it will always provide a benefit for everything it touches: those working on the project, those receiving what is made, and for scalability or adaptability once it's been created.

The Architecture of Radical Outcomes

The architecture of Radical Outcomes is the framework that helps us organize everything we create, where what we create will go, and how the pieces fit together. It is the antidote to random acts! With the structure, we can easily locate areas in need of replacement, and decide what to use to make updates. We can easily decide what is no longer relevant and needs to be discarded.

What is this architecture composed of?

START WITH THE ESSENTIAL BUSINESS OUTCOMES

All of the businesses we have ever worked with have major goals they need and want to achieve. Do they need better customer interaction? More units sold? Increased understanding of the competition? When you build an architecture, you'll need to understand the outcomes a business thrives on, so you can map them to the individual.

Those visionary outcomes require lots of different areas to be orchestrated and carried out, and need to be broken down into tangible results that someone can achieve. It's what we discuss in Chapter 5, "It's Business Outcome Time."

FACTOR IN THE AUDIENCE ENVIRONMENT

Whether in software, hardware, telecommunications, shipping, or retail, people purchase products looking to fulfill certain needs. And in a new age where customers can do their own research, read through mountains of reviews from other purchasers, or reach out to broad social networks to qualify a potential buying decision, what they expect can vary greatly. Do you know the needs of your customers, how they make decisions, and what motivates them to do business with you?

Additionally, how well do you know our audience? What is their role? What kinds of circumstances or conditions do they have in their workplace? We cover this in Chapter 7, "The Experience Is Human."

THEN – TRIANGULATE!

To create an architecture in the way that Olivia and the Oxygen team did in the conference room, you'll need to sift and sort through a lot of information and go back and forth between all the requirements. It is not a linear activity! We think of it as "triangulating" between a variety of different inputs. Figure 8.2 shows that nonlinear concept that is almost meandering, yet totally purposeful – because you are focused on the outcome.

Once you have all of these inputs, you have what you need to create a specific structure for projects, programs, and services in any given business! The architecture for Radical Outcomes is the organizing construct that helps us identify and prioritize the stuff we create. Without having a way to define (with our stakeholders) each of the areas above, it makes it really hard to know what to create, or define why we are creating it. And, as we've learned, in the absence

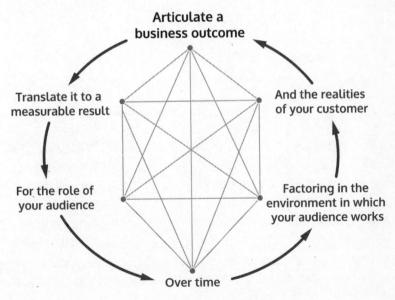

FIGURE 8.2 How to Create an Architecture for Radical Outcomes

of these considerations, it's easy for System 1 to take over and just start doing stuff.

What does an architecture for Radical Outcomes look like? Think of the documents you've seen that are architectural in nature. They aren't usually pretty to look at and can be hard to decipher unless you're really familiar with what they depict. But they are as invaluable as a Rosetta stone to guide the work of many different people. Similarly, your architecture will probably only make sense to you and the team that put it together. Figure 8.3 shows an analog example of a detailed architecture. It's messy and very preliminary.

FIGURE 8.3   Example of Detailed Architecture

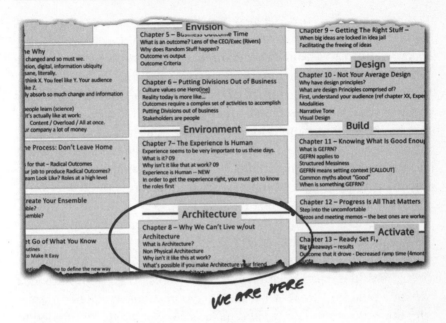

Figure 8.4 Example of High-Level Architecture

Because these kinds of artifacts can be hard to show to stakeholders, we also recommend investing in creating a high-level, polished view of your architecture. It doesn't have to be beautiful, just navigable. As you learn in Chapter 9, "Getting the Right Stuff," it's handy to have the high-level view of the architecture to be able to orient your SMEs and other stakeholders to the overall journey for your audience. Figure 8.4 shows an example of this.

When Olivia and the Oxygen team started really cranking on the whiteboard, they had reached a breakthrough moment where it was possible to take all the inputs they'd received and organize them into measurable objectives. They created Missions, which were tangible; and then underneath that, sequenced different types of activities and modalities, into episodic interactions that would leave their audience wanting more – Episodes. But it wasn't enough to make things episodic. It had to be easy for the audience to know what they needed to do next, to have a path to follow, even if their own activities on that path weren't always 100% prescribed.

That is the architecture that the team created that day.

To create an architecture for Radical Outcomes, translate business outcomes, desired results, and the environment into a set of Missions and Episodes that are sequenced, over time, in accordance with human-centered design principles.

When Olivia and the Oxygen team created the architecture, many of the myriad of inputs they'd received didn't fit. There was lots of stuff on the cutting room floor, so to speak. But now, with the architecture, there was a way to discuss *why* those items didn't make it into the architecture. They didn't serve the measurable result for the outcome, for that span of time (a program lasting 90–120 days) for the audience. So they weren't needed.

Having an architecture to drive Radical Outcomes helps you have the discussions that eliminate random acts. Instead of immediately assuming that a business's problems can be solved with training on topics, and immediately launching those topics onto your audience (which would be a System 1 reaction), you can elevate the conversation, drive to root problems, and make a suggestion that is aligned to driving the outcome, not putting a Band-Aid in place that you hope manages to be *the answer.*

It is the opposite of the chaos and disorder that characterizes random acts!

Architecture Is Indispensable to the New Way of Working

Architecture is the core component that eliminates random acts of creating stuff that we see everywhere across industries. In learning programs, enablement initiatives, or any other endeavor that seeks to equip someone in a role with new knowledge or skills, having an architecture allows you to look at content and assign it a place and clear function in the structure. What does a person in this role need to know and do to be successful? What is the best way to build that knowledge and skill?

To achieve Radical Outcomes, architecting is not just about the order of things. Architecting considers the experience that people will have, the sequence and flow of content – not just the information that needs to be given to them. Architected experience is an integral part of all our lives. Whether you are mobile ordering your coffee on the way to the office, buying groceries on Amazon, or chuckling at the joke of the day from Zappos customer service, you are having an architected experience.

Architected experiences are carefully thought through to make sure you get what you need, when you need it, with a minimum of annoyance and a maximum of positive feeling. Architected experiences make us feel that our needs are understood and that we are being helped or taken care of. Why not do this at work?

We all have an amazing opportunity to be the architects of individual and business success. The focus on experience is the fundamental reason that we talk about architecture. In a business-to-business, knowledge-worker world, thinking of the experience of your audience might seem different, or less tangible than what you experience as a consumer – yet it's just as important in order to drive business outcomes through people. And equally important to have an architecture to enable that experience.

In Chapter 9, "Getting the Right Stuff," and Chapter 10, "Not Your Average Design," we talk about how to bring the architecture to life.

Getting the Right Stuff

Try to leave out the parts that people skip.

—Elmore Leonard

Pixies. Olivia's gaze landed on the bowl of fruit on the back table, next to the different types of sugary sweet snacks, and she remembered with a smile how Marco had eaten all of the tangerines at last week's contribution session.

The room was prepared for the meeting, chairs set up in a U shape and no table in the middle. The whiteboard had a neatly drawn version of the material that had been conceived in the conference room the week before, just days before the meeting in which Marco changed his view of Olivia and her group's process. In a matter of 15 minutes, the whole scene would change: chairs would be occupied, remote callers dialed in, Jadyn projecting her screen and taking notes in real time.

The conference room door opened, and Nimit entered with Juliana and Jadyn. "Here we all are!" he announced cheerfully. "No one from Platforms here yet?"

"Not yet. But they accepted, right, Jadyn?" Jadyn nodded.

"Nice, Olivia, that's awesome," said Nimit. "Ever since last week and the big turnaround with Marco...it's great he's been able to follow up on your emails and give you the big endorsements on this process." He looked at the door. "Oh, and here are all the others from Oxygen! Goodness, you've got the whole gang here."

Aimee, Katherine, and Simon walked in, shook hands, and seated themselves near Jadyn. "I'm going to start the bridge," said Jadyn. She dialed numbers on the phone.

Callers beeped in. More people entered the room, greeting each other, shaking hands with brief small talk.

"Okay, everyone – let's get started," said Nimit. "Olivia, you want to kick things off?"

Olivia faced the room. She recognized Sanjay Prabhu, the Director of Product Management from Platforms, and next to him, also from the Platforms group, was Brad Lewellen. On the phone were three other managers from Platforms. These were all the stakeholders that Maya had said needed to be involved in contributing content. They had all kinds of know-how in their brains – all of them had been involved in the product roadmaps, had done customer implementations, and had seen the good, the bad, and the ugly. And used that feedback to shift and change their designs. Olivia felt a strange kinship with them and the iterative nature of their work, which had evolved so much over the decade.

Somehow, the Oxygen team was on one side of the room, and the Platforms SME's on the other. *Why does that always happen?* she wondered. She greeted the room, made some housekeeping remarks, then said,

"Okay, all. Let's talk about why we are here. We – "

"Yes, I can't wait," interrupted Sanjay. "Marco told me this is going to be good! I want to see this magic for myself," he grinned and looked at Brad, also grinning. He looked back at Olivia. "Though the bar is low, eh?"

Olivia had anticipated this commentary would be coming from Sanjay. Sanjay had consistently complained that all of the material coming from Jack's group had to be reworked by his people. He had lots of contact and face-time with Maya in his role, and no doubt had made his opinions known. In all honesty, she couldn't blame him, and would be thinking the same thing in his shoes. She smiled.

"Sanjay, I appreciate that. I know I can always get candid feedback from you. Always helpful."

"Happy to help, Olivia. Okay, enough joking. What do you have in store for us? I'm eager."

"Great. Sanjay, Brad, those of you on the phone . . . I'd like to walk you through how we're set up to do things differently in this meeting, certainly a change from what you're used to."

She paused as they all looked at her expectantly. "Because, I can't do my job now unless you're involved."

Sanjay looked friendly and amused. "Okay, tell us more!"

Olivia continued, gesturing at the whiteboard. "This is what we're doing. You all know the outcomes that Maya has socialized. So that is what we are all driving to, but here's the thing. I don't know what the content is because my expertise lies in how people learn, but not *what* they need to learn. The team here with me – these are the people who create the outputs. But we can't create stuff that will actually be helpful for somebody unless we know what you know, or even *part* of what you know. So, we would like to use this time with you to literally extract what you know, out of your head! You know . . . out of Idea Jail," They laughed.

"What do you think, Brad?" said Sanjay. "Is this why you haven't been able to get those Smart Devices market research findings to funding? Idea Jail, perhaps? I love that, Olivia." He paused, smiling. "Apologies. Go on."

"Well, so . . . we extract what you know, out of, yes, Idea Jail. And then, it's our job to bring it to life to make it retainable and understandable for somebody else to go do something with it."

"That sounds great!" said Brad.

"Awesome! Everyone on the phone?" Affirmations ensued. "Great! Are you ready?"

"Let's do it," said Sanjay.

"Okay, Juliana. Over to you," said Olivia.

Over the course of 90 minutes, voices spoke up, there were heated yet good-natured discussions, and the white board became populated with notes, colors, stickies, and drawings. The participants saw their tribal knowledge start to take shape in front of them piece by piece, with winding arrows and messy underlining. Olivia and Juliana volleyed ideas back and forth, facilitating discussion as the subject-matter experts chimed in. Aimee, the experience designer, chimed in with questions about the audience. Simon took notes on the projected screen in real time so everyone could see what was being documented. Jadyn looked at calendars, scheduled follow-ups, and assigned deadlines.

When the meeting had wrapped, Sanjay lingered at the door. "Olivia," he said. "That was great. My guys on the phone were messaging me. They thought it was so helpful, like someone was finally asking them what they think. Really good work."

"That's the idea," said Olivia with a smile. "We'll have the storyboard to you in 48 hours."

"48 hours. Wow. Okay, I'm going to be on a flight day after tomorrow. I'm going to use my flight time to download this and write up my feedback and then you'll get it when I land."

"Fabulous!"

When he left the room, Olivia turned back to the team. "I'd say that contribution session was a resounding success."

■ ■ ■

What role does knowledge play in innovation and change? How does the knowledge necessary to take advantage of an innovation reach the masses? When we discuss the bicycle commuters in Chapter 4, "Let Go of What You Know," we talk about all the different inputs needed to ride and steer. Even when bicycles were a completely new invention, riders learned to use them without attending public lectures and borrowing books from the library. How did they get started?

When Big Ideas Are Locked in Idea Jail

We've all seen and experienced new ideas. From clamshell cell phones to six-CD changers in cars, many products have had their own cultural heyday, however brief. When we experience innovative products, we are the beneficiaries of cumulative effort and energy that was focused on improving something, for us.

How does that process start? How does someone take stock of shifting information and begin learning new information? How do we become open to new ideas and allow the knowledge we already have to shift? What value does gaining new knowledge play in success?

In the business world, as companies shift to keep up with changing customer needs, knowledge can mean different things to different people. A software company shifts their offering, which used to be installed on desktop computers, to the cloud. What do their salespeople need to know in order to have relevant conversations with customers? A wireless telecommunications company focuses on transforming their customer service. What do their call-center agents need to do differently? A hotel chain modifies their business model to compete with the disruption caused by Airbnb. How does this impact their organization – are new roles created, and what do those people need to know and do?

All of these innovations and changes started out as ideas, Big Ideas. They are strategic decisions. And as much as our work culture and consumer-oriented expectations might desire it, there is no easy-button way to bring Big Ideas to life. As consumers, we experience the benefits of the hard work that makes innovation relevant to us, in our devices, our cars, our health, and our standard of living, but we rarely see what goes on behind the scenes to bring that idea to our doorstep. And it's hard to appreciate something that's invisible.

That's the thing about all that invisible knowledge: if someone doesn't codify it, nothing happens, and our benefit from innovation adds up to zero.

Big Ideas originate from people like Sanjay and Brad who are thinking about the future state of a system.

Whether they are scientists, engineers, scholars, or humanitarians, their life's work is applied synthesizing some piece of the future, into a big idea – a potential catalyst for change. They are often referred to in the vernacular as subject-matter experts (SMEs) and they possess deep knowledge about their domain: know-how, terminology, models, comparisons, and wisdom. And their knowledge is often incredibly hard to scale.

The SME's Dilemma

Subject-matter experts traverse a vast body of knowledge to connect ideas or invent something new. They start a new practice; create a new product or service that extends the reach of their organization; take a program and run it differently and better; or test out a new way to get things done. Some innovations might be sexier than others, but they still require big ideas to have an impact. Here are some examples:

◆ **Start a new practice.** An insurance company starts a new social-media center of excellence for engaging customers and offers this as a service for its different channels of agents.

◆ **Create something new that extends reach.** A company that originally sold books online figures out how to adapt its technology platform to become the most convenient one-stop-shop outfit on the planet, offers a tech platform to businesses, and also becomes a digital content provider. Oh, and they buy a supermarket chain.

◆ **Take a program and run it differently and better.** A large technology company that is predictably unwieldy and redundant standardizes and consolidates their sales support content.

◆ **Test out a new way to get things done.** A business merger of two entertainment firms catalyzes an opportunity for teams to unpack and understand the benefits of the creative process.

When you read a list like this, it looks pretty straightforward. That is part of the conundrum of knowledge and content: once the idea has been executed, it's easy to read about it later, looking at past impact through the lens of the present. But reading these bulleted examples still doesn't help us figure out *how* those Big Ideas came to life.

Now consider how many thousands of millions of ideas have been conceived in your business, field, or domain, to think outside the box or do things differently. Any guesses?

We can never actually know the number, because most ideas never make it into the open air from the brain where they're conceived.

WHY IT'S HARD TO TURN THE IDEA INTO REALITY

SMEs tend to constantly ruminate about building their knowledge out further. They create all kinds of new stuff: conceptual models, processes, methods, products – all manner of intellectual property.

You've seen these people before. They are the account director who brings in the largest deals; the solution architect who ends up being the reason the customer is doing business with your company; the designer who wins the awards; the prolifically published professor whose books are only understood by a select few. They have a lot of know-how and they see things beyond the status quo that other people don't see.

But SMEs struggle to translate their ideas to people who could potentially help them make that knowledge more accessible. SMEs are highly effective through their own *unconscious competence*. Their ability to create new things, and think of new ideas, is so intrinsic, that asking them to stop, take a step outside themselves, and convey what they are doing is next to impossible.

Moreover, SMEs are usually the busiest, most overburdened resources on a team or in a business. They are usually so busy doing what others perceive as magic, that they don't have the time to unpack what they are doing or how they think. Nor are they able to take time to convey their knowledge to others.

And so, their catalytic thinking enters into a vicious cycle: Only they know how to use their knowledge. So they carry the burden of doing it. In the process of doing it, they develop more ideas – but only they know how to do it. So they carry the burden even more.

Another way to think of this phenomenon is:

The knowledge of experts is shackled inside of Idea Jail.

The lockup of ideas is surrounded by irony. Idea Jail happens when an expert's unconscious competence remains tethered to them, due to the burdens placed on them by the very knowledge that makes them valuable.

Idea Jail is reinforced by an organization's culture or operating model, which may not have any processes or provisions to extract, formulate, and transport knowledge from its gurus. Idea Jail causes burnout and overwork for the SME (they end up not trusting any-one else with what they know) and a missed opportunity for the organization or cause they work for. It's a lose-lose situation.

If Sanjay and Brad were able to work with some other group consistently, a group that was focused on rendering what they know into more digestible formats, then their decades of experience can help others in their role. Their knowledge can scale. But most of the time, there is no such group to help them. Or is there?

If you have a process, as Olivia did, that helps you extract what the SME knows, and break it down into manageable components, you actually make their job easier. If you consider that expert as a source of great content that is relevant to your audience and help to extract and articulate what someone needs to know and do for a specific outcome, you ease the burden on them to constantly explain what they do.

In the business world, when it comes time to share the knowledge that helps people succeed, it's easy to get wrapped up in what you think an executive wants to hear, or what you think the right answer is. Yet it's the utility of the content for the audience that matters. Someone, or some team, needs to formulate that content so that it helps the audience drive toward a business outcome.

Freeing Content from Idea Jail

It's up to you to extract that content from the minds of the SMEs, sequence it properly, and set the right expectations for how it'll be used and represented. In the Radical Outcomes process, there's a meeting for doing this. We call these content-gathering meetings *contribution sessions.*

These sessions are critical to getting the content you need that is relevant to your audience. If you don't handle them effectively, the experience you are creating will not be successful no matter how hard you and your team work. Our team has run these sessions and seen them both succeed, as with Olivia's team, but also fail, as was the case when we worked with a telecommunications company, where we struggled to run sessions where participants got bogged down in details and didn't keep the audience in mind.

The most important aspect of these sessions is your mindset. Remember, you have to let go of what you *think* you know.

Facilitating the Process

In the rest of this chapter, you'll read about how to actually prepare for and run a contribution session, so that your SMEs feel unburdened and your content is relevant to your audience. You'll be amazed at how easy it is – and how much your SMEs will appreciate, and even look forward, to participating.

PREPARING FOR A SESSION

Start by sending an email to your SMEs well ahead of time explaining their role in these sessions. Be clear about the goals and outcomes of the project, and exactly how they will contribute.

Just as Olivia and her team had an architecture for the experience they wanted to create, you will have a similar type of artifact, in which the Missions and Episodes for each area of the architecture, which reflect a high-level view of what someone needs to know and do to achieve the measurable result, are clear and agreed upon. As you drill into the Episode topics to develop, refer to the architecture to provide context to your SMEs, and publish the agenda well ahead of each contribution session. If you created a high-level view of the architecture, as we advise in Chapter 8, "Why We Can't Live without Architecture," you can show that structure in the first slide of every meeting to show your SMEs where you are in the experience.

Document the expectations and contribution topics, right into the meeting invite. It speeds up your kickoff and also gives all attendees an easy place to reference if they need a refresher on meeting goals. Figure 9.1 shows a screenshot of the type of meeting invite we've used to make it easier for your SMEs to know what to expect.

Also, attach the Contribution Session slide deck (which we'll discuss below) to the invitation.

As you prepare, think through the roles that everyone in the session will play. How many of these people understand the new process and way of working? Chances are, your SMEs will need more explanation.

Plan to record the meeting (audio only, or video conference recording). This gives you a backup record of the conversation in case you or someone else needs to revisit any content. This is especially important if you are both facilitating the meeting and later creating the asset from the session.

USING A CONTRIBUTION SESSION DECK

The Contribution Session Slide Deck is built using a template that you customize for each contribution session. The deck is structured to open the meeting, set context, and then capture all SME input live during the meeting. The deck closes by setting expectations for the next steps.

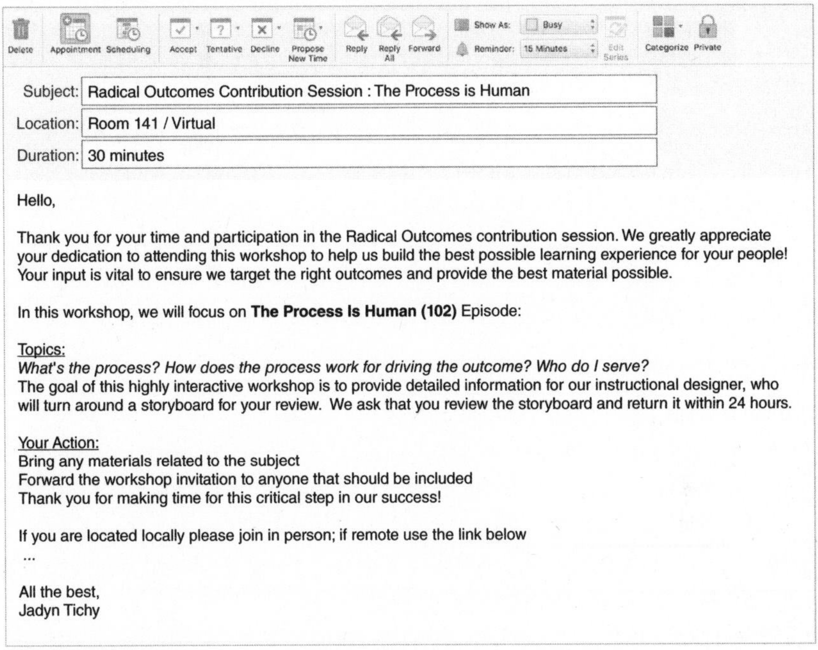

Subject: Radical Outcomes Contribution Session : The Process is Human

Location: Room 141 / Virtual

Duration: 30 minutes

Hello,

Thank you for your time and participation in the Radical Outcomes contribution session. We greatly appreciate your dedication to attending this workshop to help us build the best possible learning experience for your people! Your input is vital to ensure we target the right outcomes and provide the best material possible.

In this workshop, we will focus on **The Process Is Human (102)** Episode:

Topics:
What's the process? How does the process work for driving the outcome? Who do I serve?
The goal of this highly interactive workshop is to provide detailed information for our instructional designer, who will turn around a storyboard for your review. We ask that you review the storyboard and return it within 24 hours.

Your Action:
Bring any materials related to the subject
Forward the workshop invitation to anyone that should be included
Thank you for making time for this critical step in our success!

If you are located locally please join in person; if remote use the link below
...

All the best,
Jadyn Tichy

Figure 9.1 Example of a Meeting Invite for a Contribution Session

What to Include in Your Contribution Session Deck

- Project description
- Project definition of success
- Role of the SMEs in the meeting
- The architecture (or a user-friendly rendering of it) to show where this content fits in the overall journey
- The Episode topics to be discussed, to drive to what someone needs to know, and then *do*, to achieve the measured result
- Blank notepads for taking notes in between topics, to document the conversation
- Next steps, including storyboard turnaround time and guidelines for SME review/approval of storyboard content

Running an In-person Contribution Session

The in-person contribution session has many advantages, if all of your SMEs are located in the same place. It is possible to cover far more ground in person than using virtual meetings, and the facilitator can read body language, sense conflict, or keep people focused and prevent too much multitasking.

How Long Should a Contribution Session Be?

Contribution sessions are typically no more than 90 minutes long, and sometimes shorter depending on the availability of your SMEs. We have found that, while it can be fun, it's also hard work to go back and forth when the content is dense or complex – and for this reason, keeping sessions to this length, rather than scheduling all-day or half-day sessions, is best.

Room Setup

◆ Print or project the blueprint to show meeting attendees and orient them as to where their contribution fits into the big picture.

◆ Set up a large whiteboard or a good supply of self-sticking flip charts already hung on the walls.

◆ A projector and laptop with Contribution Session Slide Deck ready to show.

Visibility Set up the physical space so that everyone can see the whiteboard and the projector screen.

Outcomes Write the Episodes and their associated objectives on a flip chart or whiteboard to be displayed for the duration of the meeting. Having a calm and prepared environment in the room as people arrive is critical!

Snacks Bring snacks. Give people leave to munch on something while thinking, to stand up and stretch, walk around, leave for the restroom as necessary, or take an important call. Treat people like responsible adults – it builds a collaborative and collegial environment immediately.

RUNNING A VIRTUAL CONTRIBUTION SESSION

In today's working environments, it's nearly unheard of to have all the people you need in one location at any given time. Virtual meetings are the norm; so if you are meeting with SMEs virtually:

◆ Use a conference service with video if at all possible, and ask everyone to turn on their cameras. It's much more effective for

SMEs to see your face, each other, and to see the live notes being recorded on screen.
◆ Remind SMEs they can access the meeting slide deck from the meeting invitation if they want to follow along on their own computer

Unfortunately, you can't give them snacks over the internet. But let them know they can bring their own!

WHAT TO EXPECT DURING A SESSION

As the meeting facilitator, you'll need to consider:

◆ What to say to folks who doubt or question the process in the room
◆ How to keep the meeting moving
◆ When/how to redirect the conversation back toward the outcomes

Sessions can have different cadences depending on who's contributing. You may talk around topics and slowly focus in on them, or you might dive right into something linear. SMEs have a variety of approaches to how they explain their work. That means we need a variety of ways to help get the content out of their heads.

As you move through the session, you will see the content start to lay itself out on the whiteboard, flipchart, and/or in notes. It will be messy! No big deal – the point is to extract from your participants. Later, you'll have a chance to clean up and sort through the content to determine what is most relevant to your audience and when, in the life cycle of their role, the information will be most useful. Are you discussing a concept that will need to be constantly revisited for all employees? Is this a basic set of instructions for a tool that needs to be used daily? The way SMEs suggest the audience needs to use the information can help determine *when* they'll need it.

Finally, give clear expectations about turnaround. If you're using the agile method we propose, you'll build more trust with SMEs by delivering a first iteration of the content you've decided to create quickly for their validation (we normally allow a 48- to 72-hour turnaround time for first content review), before taking the content back to add more polish. The content might be a messy PowerPoint deck, it could be a video script, or a mock-up of a digital flier.

Emphasize that grammar and copyedits will be handled at the end of the project – right now the focus is getting the content (subject matter) right.

End the meeting with clear expectations about content turnaround and validation. Let them know you'll deliver a storyboard or outline (we discuss storyboards more in the Chapter 10, "Not Your Average Design") for them to review for *content only* – not design, grammar or spelling; not visual polish; not brevity or flair.

As we mentioned earlier, turnaround times for delivering a first iteration of a storyboard or content outline are important in building trust with SMEs. We normally allow a 48- to 72-hour turnaround time for first content review.

Yes, you read that right. *48 to 72 hours.* And yes – it's totally achievable, as long as you recognize that something just needs to be Good Enough for Right Now (another concept coming right up in Chapter 11) for that part of the process.

Things are going to move quickly at this point. Contribution sessions morph immediately into storyboards that contain the content that was codified with the SMEs. Once the session is done, the appointed experience designer has everything that is needed to do a first pass. It will *not* be pretty. It will *not* be perfect. It will *not* be finished. It will have roughed-out activities, or example images. It will be exactly what it is supposed to be: a first iteration.

You'll give it to SMEs for content review and to trusted colleagues for feedback on the design and activity structure. Then you'll iterate again, and again, until it's ready for Design – just in time for the next chapter!

DESIGN

Not Your Average Design

The broader one's understanding of the human experience, the better design we will have.

—Steve Jobs

The exhibition gallery was crowded that Sunday, but even so, observers maintained a quiet buzz of comments and conversation. At the far end of the gallery, there was a display case at waist level. Olivia bent forward and peered over the top, her face close to the glass. "Incredible," she whispered, then looked up at the prints on the wall, then back into the glass.

Another face appeared beside Olivia, peering into the case in a similar fashion, and then looking up at the wall. "Cool," said Olivia's sister Bernadette. "I can see why so many people were talking about this exhibit."

"I mean, look at the attention to detail. You can see all the passes he went through on the stencils, down here and here. So many different colors! But then it all comes together in the final prints."

"What I find amazing is the number of stencils he must have used. Look at the details on the waves! That's like, obsessive," said Bernadette.

The sisters straightened up together and looked at the wall, on which were hung a series of framed, unfinished prints by the Japanese artist Katsushika Hokusai. All of them showed stenciled passes of single colors, layered on top of one another, as a way of showing the progress from blank sheet of paper to finished print. The final print, *Under the Wave off Kanagawa*, was hung on its own panel to their right, where a small group of observers studied it, murmuring their thoughts. In the case were the stencils used to create the print, laid out in a sequence. "The technique is called . . . *ukiyo-e* . . . not sure how to pronounce that," said Olivia, reading a caption near the case. "The artist paints his final work of art onto paper or silk. After that, an engraver attaches the painting to a piece of wood and creates a series of stencils of the artwork." She looked at the stencils. "So the engraver had to create like 20 of these? And a different one for every color? So painstaking." She continued reading. "When the stencils are ready, they go to a printer, who places each stencil, one by one, onto paper."

"Quite the collaboration," said Bernadette. "Think of how important it is that all those people be really good at their part of the process, but also know what they are working toward."

Olivia suddenly stopped reading and stood up, then turned to look intensely at Bernadette. "What did you just say?"

"Well, I'm just saying that the final print isn't there just because of Hokusai. I mean, it is because of him, of course it wouldn't exist without his concept of it, but then, it also wouldn't exist if he didn't have an engraver and a printer who knew what they needed to do. I mean, I guess Hokusai could have been satisfied with just a painting of it, but clearly there was a thing about wood prints going on, and anyway, the final print is just such an amazing combination of mastery from the different techniques used . . . so vibrant . . . look at those waves . . . hey, what is up with you? Where are you going?"

Olivia had turned and was walking toward the door of the gallery, pulling out her phone as she walked. By the time Bernadette caught up with her, Olivia had the phone to her ear. "I have to make a call," she said quickly. They stood outside the doors to the exhibition, above which was a large painted exhibition sign that said "Hokusai: 1760–1849." A reproduction of *Under the Wave off Kanagawa* hung to the right of the doors, with its painted caption text creating a white-on-dark-green frame of Olivia's head.

"Olivia, c'mon, we were supposed to be taking a break today! You're not working, are you?"

"It'll just be a minute. Hey," said Olivia into the phone. "It's me. Guess what. I just realized something. You said the other day, 'There's no consistent branding or look and feel,' right? And we did that pass at the architecture, but now people on our team are stuck asking the same types of questions about how much information to put in a view, or the tone of writing." Olivia paused, listening. "Right, that too. It's about some kind of set of guidelines around how we write, visualize, how much is too much text." She turned and faced the wall, the pristine white text just inches from her face. Olivia raised a finger to touch the text as she spoke. *Hokusai was one of the most prolific printers, producing more than 30,000 prints in his lifetime,* said the text.

"It has to be created in consideration of the environment..." she said. *More than 30,000 prints.* After a short pause, she turned around again. "Okay, great. So we'll do a meeting on that. I agree.

"If we want the experience to be consistent and cohesive, and we want our team to be able to move quickly to do this work, we have to establish clear design principles."

■ ■ ■

A number of years ago—quite a few, in fact, that it's somewhat alarming that things haven't changed more—the data visualist Edward Tufte wrote a brief report called *The Cognitive Style of PowerPoint* (2003). In it, he shares a skeptical view of PowerPoint's propensity to offer hierarchical bullets as its prime interface for displaying information. Tufte presents an argument that shows how its simplified interface potentially shaped (or squandered) the display of complex information by leaving out critical components that other types of human interaction or visualization might otherwise have rendered. He connects this argument to an example of how information was displayed on a PowerPoint slide during an analysis of the Columbia Accident Investigation Board, with this important citation:

As information gets passed up an organization hierarchy, from people who do analysis to mid-level managers to high-level leadership, key explanations and supporting information is filtered out. In this context, it is easy to understand how a senior manager might read this PowerPoint slide and not realize that it addresses a life-threatening situation.

At many points during its investigation, the Board was surprised to receive similar presentation slides from NASA officials in place of technical reports. The Board views the endemic use of PowerPoint briefing slides instead of technical papers as an illustration of the problematic methods of technical communication at NASA.[1]

PowerPoint slides, web browser interfaces, phone apps, classroom training. What do all of these items have in common? They all are utilized to convey information, used in organizations everywhere as tools to help people learn. Yet in the example provided above, which had life-threatening implications, something critical was missing, that allowed for a situation where the information presented was not assimilated – not because it was incorrect, but because it could not be interpreted due to the *design* of how it was presented. And by not being clear about what the design needed to achieve, the outcome – based on the decisions made by NASA based on the information presented – was disastrous. Whoever created those PowerPoint slides was not working with effective design principles.

Making Information Easy to Consume

Most of the time, when we create stuff at work, the stakes are not so high nor the consequences so dire. It's been a decade and a half since Tufte published his paper, and while PowerPoint still offers bullet formats as a core part of its interface, we don't believe PowerPoint is really the problem when it comes to creating things that have real impact or usability. Frankly, PowerPoint is the *only* tool of its kind—at least for now—that has such a ubiquitous reach in the workplace to present information. It's here to stay, for the time being. So maybe it's really about how you use it – and other commonly used tools that present complex information.

What's behind this? How do you get to your goal of making an experience easy for the audience and at the same time, get everyone (you, stakeholders, and your team) on the same page as to what *good* looks like?

Throughout this book, we touch on Daniel Kahneman's concept of System 1 and System 2 thinking. One of the core determinations made by System 1 and System 2 at any given time of consciousness is where something lies on a spectrum from *cognitive ease* to *cognitive strain*. "The assessments are carried out automatically by System 1, and one of their functions is to determine whether extra effort is required from System 2."[2]

Kahneman writes about the causes and consequences of cognitive ease, which has several significant characteristics that we believe are critical in either alleviating or contributing to information overload in the workplace. Kahneman elaborates an example: "A sentence that is printed in a clear font, or has been repeated, or has been primed, will be fluently processed with cognitive ease . . . Conversely, you experience cognitive strain when you read instructions in a poor font, or in faint colors, or worded in complicated language."

He goes on to say:

> The various causes of ease or strain have interchangeable effects. When you are in a state of cognitive ease, you are probably in a good mood, like what you see, believe what you hear, trust your intuitions, and feel that the current situation is comfortably familiar. You are also likely to be relatively casual and superficial in your thinking. When you feel strained, you are more likely to be vigilant and suspicious, invest more effort in what you are doing, feel less comfortable, and make fewer errors, but you also are less intuitive and less creative than usual.[3]

Here's the interesting thing that we see in Kahneman's construct. Whether circumstances exist that result in cognitive ease *or* cognitive strain, both can produce learning. It's just a matter of what combination of System 1 and System 2 the brain invites to engage.[4] So when we design an experience for someone, we're not insisting that someone shouldn't have to experience cognitively difficult things. We do believe, however, that there's a predominance of random information given to people, that makes it incredibly difficult to consume *anything at all*. As with art, it's a balance. And, as with art, producing it requires a team of people to all be on the same page about how that experience (derived from the content extracted from their sources, including those SMEs) will be rendered. It requires – as Olivia realized in the museum – *design principles*.

Experience Design Brings Together Different Components

During her visit to the museum, Olivia realized that she and her team were missing a crucial ingredient to their ability to build the architected experience that the business needed. She realized that, even though her team and business stakeholders had made great strides in determining what a salesperson needed to know and do in order to achieve the measurable objectives that would add up to Radical Outcomes, they lacked a common set of guidelines as to how to render that subject matter, consistently and coherently. She knew that what they created in the end had to be done quickly – and in some ways, with so many different people working on it, it would be impossible to tell who actually did the work, only that it was a team that made it happen. Like Hokusai and his team of engravers and printers, everyone had to be on the same page if they wanted to reach a level of production volume and quality that stakeholders were expecting.

What goes into establishing design principles? In the previous chapter, we talk about how to get ideas and content out of Idea Jail. Once you have the information gathered in contribution sessions—either in the meeting itself or in quick iterations that follow—next you and your team must assess whether the breadth and depth of what was extracted meets the needs of the audience.

Design principles are the criteria that help you and your stakeholders make the call as to what's really needed to deliver an experience that's accessible to your audience and "meet them where they're at."

Inputs to Design Principles

Firstly, there are inputs to design principles. These inputs –which we discuss in Chapter 7, "The Experience Is Human" – are all about your audience: their work environment, their role, any requirements or constraints to be considered. If you've done the work to get to know your audience, you'll know these inputs well, and will have

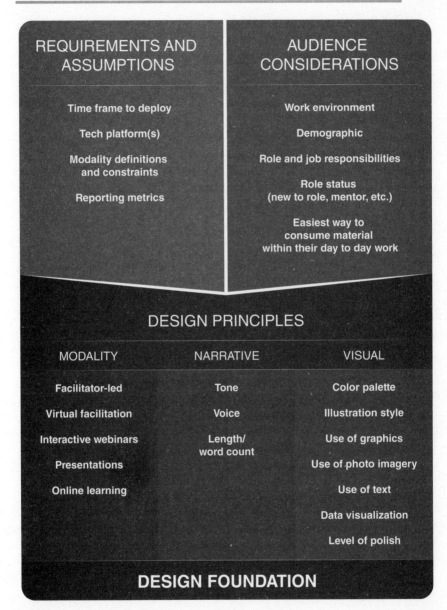

REQUIREMENTS AND ASSUMPTIONS

Time frame to deploy

Tech platform(s)

Modality definitions and constraints

Reporting metrics

AUDIENCE CONSIDERATIONS

Work environment

Demographic

Role and job responsibilities

Role status (new to role, mentor, etc.)

Easiest way to consume material within their day to day work

DESIGN PRINCIPLES

MODALITY	NARRATIVE	VISUAL
Facilitator-led	Tone	Color palette
Virtual facilitation	Voice	Illustration style
Interactive webinars	Length/ word count	Use of graphics
Presentations		Use of photo imagery
Online learning		Use of text
		Data visualization
		Level of polish

DESIGN FOUNDATION

Figure 10.1   Examples of Design Principles

discussed and validated them with your stakeholders. Figure 10.1 provides examples of these principles, though they will be different depending on your audience and the outcomes.

Requirements and Assumptions. This category of inputs might be known from the beginning, as was the case in the initiative at Omen, Inc., which imposed a three-month time line on the team. But the inputs might be unknown as well, or perhaps better stated, they might only exist in the form of assumptions. For example, one group of stakeholders might assume that all learning happens in a classroom. Another might be thinking that money could be saved by moving everything to an online platform. But what if such a platform doesn't exist at the company? Who owns that platform? Who maintains it? How will usage be reported, regardless of whether people attend workshops or sit in front of a computer? These are all the things that have to be considered at the outset, and when they're not called out or determined up front, can cause lots of downstream confusion and delays.

Audience Considerations. In Chapter 7, "The Experience Is Human," we elaborate on understanding your audience, and provide examples of the types of questions you can ask to better understand their role and environment. You certainly don't want to be in the situation where you architect an online learning path for thousands of customer service agents, only to find out that their computers don't have video cards.

COMPONENTS OF DESIGN PRINCIPLES

Some of your audience considerations will be understood well enough to shape the architecture of Missions and Episodes that you create – for instance, the role of the audience should be quite clear. Other considerations, such as their demographic, might have implications on the design principles you establish. All of these considerations will shape your design principles across three different areas: Modality, Narrative, and Visual.

Modality When we use the term "modality" we specifically refer to the delivery method of the experience. Our view in general is that experiences should be designed as multimodal so as to create variety and keep the audience engaged, interweaving different modalities through time. This isn't always possible (due to requirements and constraints – see above!), so it's best if you try to follow a few rules of thumb.

- **Live, facilitated methods** (meetings, workshops, classroom settings, even keynotes) feature activities that get people talking with each other, practicing what they are learning and moving around the room.
- **Online methods** can include a range of media types, from presentations to animations, interactive webinars, and a variety of online learning assets. Be careful of information overload when using online methods! Anything that's done online will typically need to deliver fewer bullet points of text, and launch more activities that connect people to their peers and encourage communication. We suggest limiting the amount of information and time spent in this modality to make it effective.
- **Virtually facilitated methods** (commonly known as VIL, or Virtual Instructor Led) are moderated sessions that use technology for people to participate from different locations. These methods need to ensure that people stay engaged through interactive techniques.

With any of these methods, if there's a choice available, the method should fit what someone needs to know or do. A live, facilitator-led workshop is probably overkill for certain types of knowledge, such as product information. But it can be quite effective to help with role-play or development of conversational skills, or in getting groups of people to align their thinking.

Narrative Nearly everything we create uses language and words. The style of the narrative used with the written or spoken word can make a big difference in connecting with your audience. Is the tone familiar and casual, or formal? Is the voice that of someone who is culturally familiar to the audience?

Additionally, the number of words that you put in front of your audience matters. An experience that just provides 20 bullets on a slide for 15 slides is not going to engage your audience! Even if this seems obvious, we see it over and over again and wonder: did the design team realize they were doing this? Or did they just not have a way to have a conversation about design principles, and document what was agreed to?

Visual Visual design has many components; it's no wonder we connect with the phrase, "a picture is worth a thousand words." Visually rendered information can be incredibly powerful, as anyone who is a fan of Edward Tufte will attest.

If you work in any kind of organization that has a common brand identity, you can get a head start on visual design principles by asking your marketing group for style guides or brand books. Typically these guidelines will cover the basics of visual design, such as color palette, fonts, logos, and templates for Word or PowerPoint. Some organizations will have guidelines for illustration style, use of graphics and photo imagery, or even data visualization. These can be great starting points for building off additional visual design principles for your initiative, but they often need to be augmented, as most of these brand guides tend to be fairly generic or more for a customer-facing view. To tailor the experience to your audience, you'll probably need to uncover areas that oftentimes aren't discussed. For example, think about the use of text. How much text is too much? In what situations can a graphic or image replace text? Documenting this type of more detailed criteria can help an experience designer more easily work with a visual designer to produce what's needed.

LEVEL OF POLISH

Exactly how polished does the final output need to be? Most people assume that something has to look really, really good in order to be consumable. We wouldn't disagree that it sure is nice to marvel at the level of polish of Hokusai's prints. They are truly amazing and inspiring. And – is that level of polish something that your audience absolutely requires? Or is it actually more important that the content – the subject matter – be accurate?

Level of polish or fidelity can be a tricky thing to navigate – balancing cognitive ease with other information requirements. The artists among our own team would love to see more art at work – wouldn't that be awesome? The thing is, polish is expensive, painstaking, and it's hard to change. In our experience, if you can strike a happy medium – for example, using black and white for an animation instead of full color, or reusing good, emotive imagery that's easy to license – that can go a long way toward striking that balance. Figure 10.2 shows some examples of polish: the one on the left ended up being hard to change, due to the hand in the animation; the one on the right had simple drawings

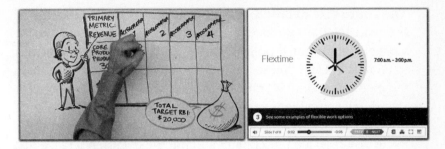

FIGURE 10.2 Examples of Polish

with motion graphics that we felt was "good enough" for what the audience needed.

COMMON MYTHS ABOUT DESIGN

We often run into situations where we talk about how the level of polish isn't really as important as the accuracy of content, and sometimes our clients get worried. *Will it look bad?* is their main concern. This is completely understandable, especially if something looking bad is a hindrance to cognitive ease.

At the same time, we still believe that there's room for compromise in the level of polish. Rather than using a video studio, one can film, "reality style," in the office. Try introducing simple graphic elements (for example, hand-drawn icons or shapes) that are easy to reproduce, but still unique.

Here are some additional myths we've run into about design and polish.

Expensive is better. Expensive is hard to change, so be really specific on where you need expensive versus a lower-cost option. Who is the audience? Will it make a difference to them? Does this asset need to be changed frequently? These are all questions to ask when thinking about the investment to make on a specific item.

The assets and production need to be super-shiny and high fidelity. Be careful here about going overboard. Did you need that level of polish applied? Did you ask the questions about polish above before deciding? See the left-hand side of Figure 10.2 for an example of "too much polish" to maintain.

The content is detailed and exhaustive. This will probably be overload for the intended audience. Too much content can be worse than too much polish: hard to update, hard for the viewer to understand and digest, and unretainable. We like to say "what's the bare minimum for someone to grasp the concept, be able to start doing something with it, and give them the ability to go find out more as needed?" Doing that mental review of content helps to cut down on a lot of content and put the details in a place that is easy to find.

Establishing Design Principles Helps a Team Decide What's Good Enough

When you start discussing these different details with your stakeholders, with inputs from your audience and the outcome that is being driven, you'll start to see patterns emerge around design principles. By agreeing on design principles, you can uncover different expectations, and then ensure that what is going to be produced is clear for everyone. The level of detail around these principles might seem mind-numbing to some, but without guidelines, you increase the risk of rework. This detail also aids the team in producing things that are coherent across assets, and with a consistent voice for the audience. One of our clients said that success meant not knowing which designer created the asset. If you have to scale, design principles are not a "nice to have," they are imperative.

The very important implication of design principles is that they essentially define what *good* looks like (see Figure 10.3). And knowing what's good – or even good enough for right now – is what the next chapter is all about.

FIGURE 10.3   Our Own Rendering of Hokusai's *Under the Wave off Kanagawa*

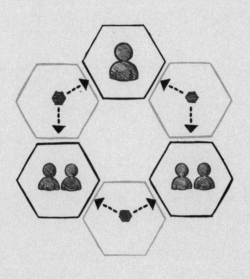

BUILD

Knowing What Is Good Enough

Don't wait for things to be perfect before you share them with others. Show early and show often. It'll be pretty when we get there, but it won't be pretty along the way. And that's as it should be.
—Ed Catmull, author *of Creativity, Inc.*

"Hey, Liv. Sorry I'm late. I just never seem to be able to finish what I'm trying to do on the book." Bernadette gave her sister a brief hug as she walked into Olivia's apartment. "And I really can't stay long."

"Whatever works for you, Dette. It amazes me that you were even able to get away last Sunday to go to the museum," said Olivia.

"Sundays are really the only days where things are remotely not insane, it's true. Kevin takes the kids...you know..."

"Yes, and, you know I've said we could meet at your place so you wouldn't have to drive over here," said Olivia.

"...Yes, and, you know I've said there is no way we are going to hang out at my house. I don't want you looking at what a disaster my study is, and telling me how I can organize it if I just do one of those work things you're always talking about," said Bernadette, smiling. "Last time it was architecture. Or was it architecture principles? At the museum?"

"It was design principles," said Olivia. "Here," she said, handing an iced coffee to her sister. "Cheers. To caffeine."

"Cheers. This must be my third cold brew today." Bernadette took a sip. "Ooh. Strong." She looked at Olivia. "So what's the buzz this week? More superhuman work?"

"This week was all about agility. We did all the storyboards for the experience."

"I think I know what you mean. But not sure. Storyboards like illustrations?"

"Here, I'll show you." Olivia walked into her home office, where the walls were papered with printouts.

"Here we go. Check this out. Looks like a bunch of slides with loads of text. Oh, and clip art," said Bernadette, putting her finger on one of the pages. She looked at the walls. "So this is where the magic happens."

"Sort of. You should see the war room at the office. And...the clip art is just a placeholder."

"So then, what happens to all this?"

"Well, it's totally iterative – I mean, this stuff here on the wall, I just put it up here today to do a quick pass on the design. But we go back and forth sometimes three times a day with revisions. Look, here's one that's almost done and programmed." She pulls up a document on her computer monitor that shows a photograph with a navigation button.

"Oohh – that looks cool. Love the background photo – wow, nice integration with text. You always were a stickler for not putting too much text in front of people. So someone just clicks their way through this?"

"Eventually, yes. We are just getting the navigation menus done so it's easy to tell where you are. But the program isn't just stuff someone does in front of a computer. They have to go do stuff too. Meet with people, have a specific type of conversation..."

"How many of these – what do you call them – are you creating?" asked Bernadette.

"Episodes. We call them Episodes. Maybe 45. Each with their own set of graphic assets, scripts, animations, work books, guides..."

Bernadette whistled. "Whew. That is a *lot* of stuff. I don't know how I would track all of that."

"Well, actually, you are tracking a lot of stuff, like in your head. For your book," said Olivia.

"Or really it's on sticky notes and books and papers strewn around my study."

"Yeah... no one knows the method to your madness except you."

"Hey, this is what it's like in academia. Publish or perish. I don't have the luxury of an army of people all doing the work for me," said Bernadette.

"Dette, that's not how it works. I don't have an 'army.' It's a small team really. We're just..."

"Go ahead, say it! You're just really productive, whereas my one-woman show of trying to write an academic tome is just putting all the burden on me. I know, creative process. I read that book you gave me by that guy who runs Pixar. It is totally cool stuff, I'll admit. How creative teams work, how they made movies like *Toy Story* and *Incredibles*..."

"I love that book," said Olivia.

"I liked it," said Bernadette. "I am just not sure how I'd apply it..."

"I get it," said Olivia. "Your book is different from my work... you're surrounded by the experts in your field who have all this specialized knowledge, so that if each chapter isn't meticulously and thoroughly researched across every possible nuance, they'll call you out for being intellectually dishonest, or find some other way to throw you under the bus..."

Bernadette nodded. "It's a jungle. Is there more cold brew?" They went into the kitchen and refilled their glasses. "That stuff in your office is cool, Olivia," said Bernadette. "To see the work in progress."

"That's all it ever is. In progress. Even the stuff that's 'done' will get changed."

"I just can't even conceive of doing my book that way. Everything has to be so buttoned up, or people will just pounce all over it. And it's not even that people are looking to discredit it – though some are – it's more that all the work other people have done is also so deep and detailed, and we're all in the same circle. And I don't know, expectations are just sooo heightened, it's like Hey, teach these two classes, *and* write these articles, *and* finish your book, *and* do these symposia. As if there's an app for all that," Bernadette said wryly.

"Yeah, I don't know, maybe it's just a different world," said Olivia. "For us, we had to extract knowledge right from the people who have done a certain job, to teach someone else how to actually do it, using the 15 years of knowledge from the first guy, but not all 15 years – just the 'best-ofs.' And render it really fast. There's no time to nitpick. We have to be really nimble and get feedback like, right away, and ask, 'Hey is this one thing accurate?' or 'Do these three things fit together right?' and we don't worry at all, not one bit, about whether it looks good yet. Until we get all the content right, then we start working on that view, what you saw on the computer."

"I can't even imagine our department working like that. They'd all be like, 'that logic is too simplistic,' or 'Why didn't you factor in the work of that team from Yale?'"

"Yeah, that's not helpful," said Olivia. "Maybe it's different outcomes. We did have to spend some time coaching people who weren't familiar with the fast turnarounds, and help them understand what kind of feedback we were looking for. And what to ignore because it wasn't ready yet. And we did have one or two people on our team who felt really uncomfortable showing work they thought was incomplete. As if they thought they'd be judged harshly."

"Which if it were my world, they'd be right to be worried," said Bernadette.

"Like I said ... maybe it's different outcomes. It's hard – everyone is so used to instant gratification, or having all the answers, like you can just ask your phone or something." Olivia jiggled the ice in her glass.

"Still," said Bernadette, "I really like those ideas. I can imagine how it takes the pressure off to be perfect. Man, that would be nice. I should really think about how that could work for me." She takes her glass, half finished, over to the kitchen sink and dumps the rest. "Too much. I'm all jitters now. And I really should go soon. Can I use your bathroom?"

Olivia returned to her home office and looked at the printouts on her wall. After a few minutes, Bernadette joined her. "What's that phrase you talk about with all this? Doesn't have to be perfect, or something?"

Olivia smiled. "Good Enough for Right Now," she said.

"That's it! Good Enough for Right Now. I really like that," said Bernadette. "That's great." She looked at the papers on the wall. "It is true, in the Pixar book, they were doing stuff that was far more audacious than this book I am writing. Maybe there's hope for me."

"Maybe just try out the idea with something small, like one of your articles. And see if it works for you," said Olivia.

"You bring up good points, sis. Doing good things. Maybe I should try to learn more stuff from you. I have to run. I'll call you this week."

Olivia nodded, then turned back and touched one of the printouts. "I think this one's GEFRN," she said.

■ ■ ■

Who among us has not seen a film created by Pixar? Who among us has failed to appreciate, or even be blown away by, the way so many complex elements had to converge in order to give us that unique experience of *The Incredibles*, not to mention *Incredibles 2?* The blending of characters, familiar voices, story, humor, music, visual design, references to things we might know, from the most overarching elements to the most minute details, all were artfully and expertly blended together into a work of art.

As consumers of all that the modern world has to offer us, we have the immense privilege of being able to enjoy these kinds of polished experiences, 24/7. We can watch bold computer-animated feature films in the theater on a screen as thin as a pencil. We can order kitchen supplies through a smart speaker perched next to the blender and take phone calls with tiny computers worn on our wrists. All of these physical, tangible things that we experience every day represent a staggering amount of money, human effort, and focus to create and make available to us. Just think of how much it cost to produce *The Incredibles*, or to engineer the smartphones now attached to our person at every waking moment.

The presence of so many wonderfully designed, meticulously engineered objects in our daily life is great . . . and at the same time, how often do we take the time to consider what might have been messy, incomplete, or complex in that process? Moreover, how does the presence of so much polish in our life contribute to a sense that everything we, too, produce, must also be polished, complete with all of the answers?

Consider the quote by Ed Catmull at the beginning of this chapter. We love Catmull's book, *Creativity, Inc.*, because of his insistence that nothing Pixar ever created was polished...when it first started. He weaves different stories of the struggles and messiness that abounded as teams of people worked together, not just to create one great film, but to figure out a way of working that could allow Pixar to create one great film after another.[1]

The insights he conveys in his book appear to be similar to what is known and practiced by the businesses who are behind today's feats of engineering or technology, be they Amazon or Apple. While it might feel like magic to those of us experiencing what they provide, it's not. *People* created the ability to order online, to get breakfast on the way to work, and the intuitive device that is used to procure that experience. But as Olivia and her sister experience, when they each enter their respective worlds of work, there can be a wide variance between the polish of their experiential world, and how they feel about their own work.

Granted, there is a big difference between *The Incredibles* which, once released back in 2004, did not undergo multiple changes to keep it relevant, and the operating system on our phone, which absolutely must constantly change or we would cease to use it. Some things do reach a level of completion that is final, because that's part of the design. Films, sculptures, and crown jewels don't tend to morph over time. Buildings can and do. Jazz performances, bicycle commutes, and the recipe for short ribs will change often, or even every time.

The stuff we create at work is somewhere in between. There's just one key idea that is the deciding point for when to share progress or call something "ready for release:" Is it Good Enough for Right Now?

What Fuels Our Need to Have All the Answers?

Perhaps there's something psychological at play, when we use such amazing technology every day, that we feel, as Olivia's sister Bernadette does, as if we must also produce deliverables whose end state can be conceived, articulated, and presented to others as finished products. Somehow, if someone shows a work in progress, it might be seen as unprepared, unfinished, messy, requiring more work...and further, that those characteristics of progress are *bad*.

We disagree. With so much complexity to deal with at work, with so many variables, nuances, and perspectives, people impacted, conflicting requirements, systems, processes, tools, and audiences, it's impossible for any one person to have all the answers for the outcomes we need to support. And in fact, the consequence of *not* allowing the sharing of unfinished, messy work can be quite dire, because we might gloss over important details that would impact the outcome.

Maybe we need to explore why we feel so uncomfortable showing work in progress, when progress is really all that matters in the path to an outcome.

If there's one thing that makes us all squirm, it's the fundamentally human fear of being wrong. Being wrong represents a threat to our self-esteem, in which we might be judged, cast out, disregarded, or deemed unworthy. Author Kathyrn Schultz describes our perception of error as "evidence of our gravest social, intellectual, and moral failings."[2] It is so stricken with negative associations that some folks will go well out of their way to defend what they think is right, even in the face of logic, science, reason, or death. Or perhaps, in a less dire sense, it's just the negative association that we have with getting feedback about our work, where we see feedback as a comment or judgment on a person and their capabilities.

If you think about it, sticking to one point of view in the face of a changing world not only makes it hard to adapt – it also is a lot of work. And to what end?

What would happen if we let go of being right and instead, recognized the benefit in not having the answer? What if we could invite inquiry, discussion, and multiple perspectives in the service of an outcome? What changes when we accept possibilities for change instead of defending the way we have always done something?

It's definitely a different way to look at error. Kathryn Schultz again:

> Far from being a sign of intellectual inferiority, the capacity to err is crucial to human cognition. Far from being a moral flaw, it is inextricable from some of our most humane and honorable

qualities: empathy, optimism, imagination, conviction, and courage. And far from being a mark of indifference or intolerance, wrongness is a vital part of how we learn and change. Thanks to error, we can revise our understanding of ourselves and amend our ideas about the world.[3]

We think this view of error is pretty awesome and liberating. And it's what we embrace when we follow the Radical Outcomes process.

What it means for the way we work is that we are constantly showing our progress, or even lack thereof. We say, "We don't have the answer. Let's go figure it out together." Then we open up the conversation. And some of it looks messy. But that's okay, as long as everyone has the outcome in mind.

We acknowledge that this is a really different mindset to have on a deliverable, and probably very difficult for someone in Bernadette's situation to change the minds of others in her department. Rather than feeling the pressure to have all the answers, it's a mindset that is curious, and open to feedback. Rather than setting our creation in stone, we can update, change, and continue to make it easier to use and better than the previous version. In that sense, it's a lot more like the technology we use every day, the updates that we receive on our phones and computers, where someone is constantly working on keeping our experience relevant.

Good Enough for Right Now Is All You Need – Right Now

Good Enough for Right Now (GEFRN – pronounced "gef-ERN") is deeply connected with the idea of moving fast in a nonlinear way that is made possible through the creation of architecture, which we describe in Chapter 8, "Why We Can't Live without Architecture." Working in this new way requires iteration on the way to a minimally viable product that is published for people to use and consume. Many of us are not used to working this way and showing progress that is messy, incomplete, or that needs more work. However, if we don't allow ourselves to share what's GEFRN, we might end up creating something that's not usable. Talk about being wrong! If we are too caught up in having all the answers, and don't check in with others who might know something that we missed, how would we know what to tweak or change?

AMAZON THINKS GEFRN – SO CAN YOU

In his 2018 letter to shareholders, Amazon CEO Jeff Bezos described his company's approach to presentations. There's no PowerPoint – instead, teams are required to present highly structured, six-page memos. And the best memos are the ones in which teams iterated and took the time to show each other their work along the way.[4]

When the team designed the architecture with Olivia, they didn't map it in a spreadsheet, call it finished, and ding anyone who strayed from the way of working. They made time within meetings and working time to consider the work together. They changed handoff processes between designers and developers when necessary, merged smaller deliverables together when it made sense, and broke larger ones out into more consumable content when the initial result was 60 minutes of talking-head content and reading. They operated as a team expecting to tweak the way they work as the tasks, projects, and outcomes changed.

GEFRN Happens Throughout the Work

The idea of GEFRN is something that we constantly think about, no matter where we are in our work. It applies to a variety of different types of interactions – so many that it will fascinate and amaze you to see what happens when you think this way. We apply it to conversations, meetings, presentations, visual renderings, really everything we work on. It's not just about deciding what's released at the end, whether it's an online experience, facilitated meeting, or executive business case. It's also a decision point for when to share work with others – a concept, an idea, or a work in progress. And the more specialized or complex the subject matter is, the harder it is to declare something GEFRN.

Of course, at some point we all individually need solitude or isolation to get certain types of work done. Writers, researchers, creative designers, or subject matter experts need to be able to use their depth of knowledge or experience to formulate, noodle, render, perhaps more like in Bernadette's world. And, if it's extremely clear who the audience is, oftentimes people can get the work done by themselves *and* be quite successful. We've seen books written, dissertations completed, deals won, paintings created pretty much through the effort of one person with some peripheral involvement by a team. And hey, if it's relevant to the audience, then no harm done. Right?

We would say, though, that such a way of working is not so effective if the audience is variable, or if the outcome requires the perspectives of people from multiple domains, or the environment is changing and causing complexity. It's especially dangerous to expect this kind of solo success with what you're working on needs to scale and reach thousands (or millions!) of people. In those situations, teaming is the way to work, and GEFRN is the way to make the call, share, get input – or go live.

It Might Look Messy, but It's Structured!

Perfection is an illusion that, in reality, is way too big of a burden for any one person to carry. Letting go of the idea that something must be perfect is incredibly liberating, similar to the emancipation we can feel when we embrace error: it makes the acts of doing, creating, and producing much easier. And, as we've said, we have no problem showing work in progress that might look messy, incomplete, or inelegant.

Just because work in progress looks inelegant does not mean it lacks structure. Far from it, the approach to achieve Radical Outcomes is specifically designed to ensure that no matter what, we are focused on the outcome, and that the messiness or inelegance of wherever we might be within the process is understood to be temporary. It involves a kind of vigilance from each of us, where we check ourselves – especially when we are feeling stressed – and ask one another to help gauge this potential desire to go beyond GEFRN.

In those moments, we ask a colleague: *is it me, or is this good enough? I can't quite tell right now.* We find that when you engage and ask one another, it enables you to either make a change, or get the thing out to its next iteration (or release). Even for major releases, we always keep in mind that whatever we create, there's a 99.99% chance that it can be adapted later on, either as a new release, or repurposed into something else. Keep in mind, if you get too attached to your output, it can get in the way of being able to help your audience. When you're open to change, feedback, and iteration, it can be very freeing.

The architected approach makes GEFRN possible. Because we have plans that identify the outcomes and clearly delineate the tasks and efforts needed to achieve those outcomes, we can always examine the individual segments that may need tweaking in the future. Working with our clients, we can hand off these project blueprints confidently to clients knowing that as customer demands reshape business outcomes, they will be able to follow the architecture to update and replace as necessary. Though each iteration itself is GEFRN, the quality of the work can slowly improve over time as teams become more and more familiar with how to get to Radical Outcomes.

As we've mentioned, most versions of the stuff you create along the way will look incomplete and kind of messy – until the last iteration or two. Kind of like what's in Figure 11.1.

You can then see the final view of the animation, as shown in Figure 11.2.

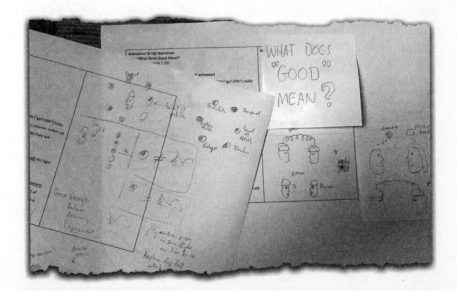

Figure 11.1 Example of a Sketch That Later Became an Animation

FIGURE **11.2** The Final Animation Based on the Sketch

FRAMING OUT GEFRN FOR FEEDBACK

While the idea of GEFRN can really lift the pressure we put on ourselves to present something as finished, we also have to make sure that the people with whom we are sharing progress are aware of what they are about to see. Framing out what's going on with an output, what stage it's in, and what kind of feedback you need is very important – otherwise you may find people providing input that isn't helpful for that iteration. For example, if you are trying to verify the accuracy of subject matter (content), or trying to work on the logic of a layout, then commenting on color choice or typos is premature.

Framing out the idea of GEFRN is particularly helpful when showing storyboards to subject matter experts. Set context with your SMEs so that they are focused on validating the information you're presenting – after all, you want to spend your time together making sure the audience understands what a technical term means, not whether or not you've used the incorrect version of *there*, *it's*, or *lets*. Instead, set the context by sharing that what you're creating will go through a copyediting pass once the content has been verified and deemed accessible for the audience.

With that kind of a context and set up, it's then easy to get people to comment on what you need to keep making progress, and you can steer the meeting away from things like polished look, punctuation, grammar, or basic visuals.

When Is Something GEFRN?

Let's think specifically about that moment where you want to make the call and share your work or release your deliverable. What does "Good" in GEFRN really mean? And who gets to decide what that means in a more tangible sense?

When it comes to the end deliverable and creating something that's relevant to our audience and that is tied to a business outcome, the ultimate rule of thumb is that *we alone don't decide what good is* – the decision is made through conversation with our stakeholders, in the interest of the audience. This can feel uncomfortable, especially if you're used to doing the majority of work on your own. Perhaps you have felt like you had to be a mind-reader for your audience or stakeholders. Or maybe others on your team had a strong point of view about what good looks like. Sometimes, you or your team may have to let go of personal preferences about what Good means, so that you can deliver what is going to work for the audience – and this determination is made through the discussions and engagement of all involved.

Progress Is All That Matters

Progress, of the best kind, is comparatively slow. Great results cannot be achieved at once; and we must be satisfied to advance in life as we walk, step by step.

—Samuel Smiles, author and politician

Walking out of the war room, Olivia's phone chimed. Voicemail. She let out a noise of exasperation at the lack of cell signal in the conference room, then played it with the phone to her ear.

"Hey, it's me," Jack's voicemail sounded tinny with a lot of background noise. "You should have an invite for today at 3 p.m. I won't be there but you and Nimit should be able to provide an update. I gotta say... I would have thought you'd be much further along by now. I know the deadlines are tight, but what the heck are you guys doing? One sec." More background noise. "Anyway, I'm sure Maya will have lots of questions for you. She told me she might be running late, but wants you to present the work you've done. So...brrrt... kkk...ga..." Jack's voice broke up and became undecipherable, then the message ended.

Olivia's stomach tensed. 3 p.m.? *That's in a little over two hours*, she thought. She turned around and went back into the conference room.

"3 p.m.? That's in two hours!" echoed Amalia. Amalia, who Olivia had hired just two months earlier, had been working with Jadyn on coordinating and managing the 1,000 different bits and pieces of the build. "I mean, I could show the status report..."

"That's not enough of an executive view," said Nimit. "Too much detail. She's already seen the walking deck. You know her, Olivia. She remembers everything, she's going to want to see progress..."

"It'll be next week before we have any demo available," said Jadyn, looking at her schedule.

The anxiety in the room became palpable as the group discussed options. Talking volumes increased.

Olivia put her hands near her ears, and turned to look around the room, at the walls of paper, the tracker tool projected on the wall. *Pixie tangerines*, came the involuntary thought into her head.

"Hey. Guys." She turned back around quickly. "Time out." The discussion abated suddenly.

"Amalia. Can you modify the location of the meeting?" Amalia nodded. "Great. Change it to this room."

"What?" said Marvin from his corner. It being a Friday, he was wearing a T-shirt and jeans. The T-shirt had a logo on it for Prank Brewing Company, with a PR inside of a rectangle, imitating an element in the periodic table. "You're going to invite Maya to this? In here? But we still have so much to figure out. We can't – "

"We can," said Olivia firmly. "Look around, guys. Look at what we are doing in this room. This is reality." She walked over to the wall, which contained long banners of paper with circles, squares, writing, all stuck to the paper.

"Olivia, it looks like a kindergarten in here..." Nimit started to say.

"And so?" said Olivia. "What is so wrong with showing progress of the actual work being done? And to share with her some of the things that we haven't figured out yet? And, I respectfully disagree about the kindergarten thing. One, kindergarten is probably the place where we humans learn the most – wouldn't it be great if we could learn like that now? Two, I challenge you to find five-year-olds who could organize all of this." She gestured around the room.

The room was silent.

"We didn't *create* this complexity, you guys. Any more than... than..." she pointed at Marvin's T-shirt. "Any more than people created hydrogen when they assembled the periodic table."

"Now, that's a new one, Olivia," said Nimit.

"Seriously, guys. Hydrogen always existed. The periodic table just organized something that already existed. We are doing the same thing! All the complexity – all the inputs we've had to sort through, and synthesize. All the different people we've had to meet with – to validate and assemble the architecture." She walked over to the paper-covered wall. "All this! We did this! It was hard!" She picked up printouts that are on the table. "The contribution sessions – the storyboarding – it's a ton of details. But someone has to do it. We can't make that complexity just go away, and come up with some answer. This is reality!"

"Hydrogen isn't the most complex element there is...actually it's quite simple...one proton, one electron...at least in its atomic structure..." said Marvin.

"Okay, whatever – so maybe it's not the best analogy. C'mon guys, let's really understand the point here. Our business is complex, and did we, or did we not, resolve to *not* add more random stuff into the mix?"

People began to nod.

"And do we agree that we have to manage all this complexity if we want to create something relevant for the sellers? Or find a way to translate it, prioritize it?"

"And explain to the SMEs why something is included or not..." said Nimit.

"So then, why not just show it all to Maya? Let her see the complexity, and let's have a conversation about it, and where we're stuck. For example – that one episode where the sales SMEs wanted to include all that content for opportunity reviews? And we had to push back and say, 'That's too much for one human being to digest in a 10-minute vignette?' And then we finally got them to agree to the three things that someone needed to know, in their first 90 days. Then, we were able to redesign it to spread the content out over time."

More nods.

"Guys..." Olivia slowed down. "We don't have to have the answers for her."

Nimit stood up, suddenly aligned. "We just have to show her what progress looks like. And let her know how she can help."

"Exactly," said Olivia. "So here's how we could start the discussion..."

• • •

Step into the (Temporarily) Uncomfortable

Whether in school or the work environment, we've all been in situations where we're expected to show work that's perfect and high quality. And while we might question whether something can ever really be perfect, there are plenty of situations where the work has to be, if not high quality, the *right* quality for the objective at hand.

In a complex environment, getting to Radical Outcomes using the iterative approach can feel very uncomfortable at first, and can take some getting used to – both for you and your team, and also for your stakeholders. As we discuss in Chapter 11, "Knowing What Is Good Enough," we cringe at the possibility that we might be wrong about something – or that our work doesn't provide the whole answer. It can feel as though our credibility and reputation are on the line.

But just as Olivia realized when she was under pressure to provide an update to Maya, oftentimes it is simply impossible to have the whole answer, packaged and ready to go. With all of the complexity that had to be managed, simple answers or polished deliverables weren't going to simply materialize out of thin air, even though many of Olivia's stakeholders had been conditioned to have that expectation. Olivia and her team had to do a lot of difficult, upfront work to envision the outcome, understand their audience and their environment, and architect a path for the audience, for which her team would create only that which was feasible to consume. Typically, it's this upfront work that is often invisible to stakeholders. And yet, it has to happen. Think of it this way: If the answer were so simple, wouldn't it be implemented and working right now?

Steve Jobs once said, "Simple can be harder than complex. You have to work hard to get your thinking clean to make it simple. But it's worth it in the end."[1] We believe this statement is, in itself, a paraphrase that was probably synthesized from a much longer point of view, but its point is profound. Somebody has to do the work of confronting the complexity and figuring out what will match the outcome. Anything less will just continue to propagate the random things that waste your company's money.

It's within this work, the tough job of sorting through lots of complexity and variables, that iteration plays its amazing role. Iteration is a two-way street: try something fast, and get feedback. Based on the feedback, recalibrate and continue. Repeat until it's GEFRN.

If you're not used to doing iterative work like this, though, then putting an idea out there when it's still rough can feel quite unnatural. System 1 wants to make it easy and serve up the answer, but System 2 needs to be engaged to do the work. It's a vulnerable place to be – and understandably so. You and your team might feel like a judgment is about to descend about people's capabilities or intellect. It's a place where people can really take things personally if they perceive their work isn't "done."

Recall Hal Crook's quote at the beginning of Chapter 2, "The Process: Don't Leave Home Without It": "Since the process of practicing and learning continues throughout your entire lifetime without ever reaching completion, this process is all there is." While we might think a seasoned jazz performer has reached the top of their game or the pinnacle of perfection, the fact of the matter is that *they* believe there is still more work to be done. It's all relative. So, why not let go of the idea that you must have the answer, and allow iteration to bring everyone in on the fun?

Iterating with a team requires setting up an environment in which people feel it is safe to iterate. We discuss these teaming aspects in Chapter 3, "Create Your Ensemble." Iteration – with or without stakeholders involved – means setting the expectation that feedback is really just ideas that add up to progress, not about any one individual's capabilities or intellect. And it requires a mindset of receptivity – where you can truly geek out on feedback, because that's what brings something to its GEFRN state, and allows for it to continuously improve over time.

In our work with clients, we rely on iteration. Without it, there is very little chance that one person could get the asset produced to a specification that is going to help the audience. Getting feedback and doing small and fast iterations that make progress with many inputs helps to ensure whatever is finally produced is going to push the outcome along.

By contrast, the traditional way of working can feel incredibly heavy and burdensome. Have you, or someone on your team, taken the whole burden of creating an output alone, then experienced that "oh no" moment of realizing, right before the deadline, that something isn't going to hit the mark? And the undeniable frantic rush to produce what's needed? When you iterate with your team or stakeholders working backwards from deadlines and outcomes, of course – things will make progress through time in smaller increments, faster.

And, to your stakeholders, progress is really all that matters. Provided they can actually see it.

Showing Iterative Progress Can Be Messy

When Olivia decided to bring Maya into the war room and show her what the team was really doing, she had really taken a major step to demystify the process of confronting complex realities and allowing visibility into just how messy things can get. The average consumer doesn't typically see all the design debates about what will go into the next iPhone, or just how many prototypes it takes to change the form factor of a laptop. But the average consumer isn't running that business. Is it better for an executive like Maya to be shielded from all the details that are the true representation of her business, or to have some visibility into what's going on to make improvements? Perhaps she might even have some insight to offer.

The challenge of showing progress within a messy part of the process is, well, it's messy (see Figure 12.1). So the typical methods of moving a diamond along a Gantt chart, or showing nice, shiny outputs, might not convey just how much progress is being made. This makes Olivia's decision to invite Maya into the conference room that much more insightful. It's like a tour of the factory floor!

In Olivia's case, her idea was to shift the expectation – both for her team, who thought they needed to "have the answer" – and for Maya, who presumably would have been thinking, "where's my answer" – and pivot to something completely different. You might

FIGURE 12.1   Progress Shown as Storyboards

find yourself in this same situation. What if you could say, to a Maya-like person, "Hey, here's the progress we're making against the solution and the outcome. Right now we're in the middle of step 4 of our process, Design. Previously, we had to sort through a lot of inputs to create our architecture; you can see the evidence of all that work here on the wall. Here are some of the places where we're stuck, for these reasons. What do you think?"

Oftentimes, you won't have the opportunity to invite someone into your production room to show them what's going on. So it's important to also understand what someone might expect to see in terms of progress, and ways in which you can communicate progress so that you're conveying what's happening in reality. How do you do that?

Communicating Progress Requires Structure, and a Point of View

Recall the concept of Idea Jail, from Chapter 9, "Getting The Right Stuff." To a certain extent, we all have some ideas in Idea Jail, and struggle to get them out. The same can be said about showing progress when we are dealing with lot of complexity. We all know highly capable people who exert superhuman efforts to manage something complex, and do all the work "in their head." That might be just fine for one project, but when you're dealing with orders of magnitude more scope or scale, then structure is needed to get a team of people on the same page. The structure that we recommend is the Radical Outcomes process, articulated in Chapter 2, "The Process: Don't Leave Home Without It," which provides a way for you to show what's being done at every stage.

How you decide to "show what's being done" is an interesting information rendering challenge, and it depends on the type of view that your stakeholders are used to seeing. Do they like to get updates via email? Or a regularly occurring phone call? How about sitting in on a daily sync?

Regardless of the method you use to communicate progress, it's important to make sure that all stakeholders know about your process, at least at a high level. They need to know *what* the process is, of course – its stages and outputs – and more important, they need to know *why* the process is important.

The opening chapter of this book explained *why* we need to think in terms of Radical Outcomes. This message is something that can help you develop a point of view to communicate within your own organization. Why have a process? Why iterate? Why is it ok to not have all the answers right away? Once people know why you're doing things differently, it can be very powerful for bringing naysayers like Marco on board, and also to create the environment where Olivia could show a stakeholder a lot of work in progress.

We outlined at the beginning of the book why the process is important – without it, complexity overtakes structure, and prevents people from focusing on the outcome. Upfront work, critical for developing an architecture, falls by the wayside or is ignored. Take some time to think about this point of view, and see what kinds of small iterations you can do to see how it resonates in your organization.

Tips for Showing Progress

Show your work early and often. In case you hadn't realized it, we believe in lots of revisions and iterations. Take a look at the hard drive for someone on our team, or in the version history of our online tools, and you'll likely find 15, 20, or 25 versions of an output that's been posted, modified, or commented on. Iterations and revisions should follow a frequency of days, or even hours, not weeks. A rule of thumb is, if you're not turning something around fast (hours or one to two days), you might be taking on too much for the iteration.

Need to show this kind of progress to a stakeholder? We love screenshots that tell the story of "Look at how this output evolved from an ugly storyboard to this design concept that's almost ready for polish."

Most important, do not go into radio silence for six weeks and then emerge from your cave saying something is finished. It's not finished if it's not iterated.

What Are Some of the Tools We Use to Show Progress?

We can't really escape the need to be able to codify progress and show it to stakeholders. So when it comes to the tools we use, some of them are actually fairly commonly used, others are a bit more unconventional. When combined with the right process, though, stakeholders can easily stay apprised of what's going on.

- ◆ **Status reports and Gantt charts.** Yes, we use these. They are only as good as the information that's shown in them, and the process they convey. Different organizations will have tools that are commonly used, and we find that, for the most part, the tools from the *Project Management Body of Knowledge (PMBOK)*[2] are useful as long as they aren't trying to serve up – you guessed it, the whole answer.
- ◆ **Detailed tracking tools.** We use Excel spreadsheets and online spreadsheets like Smartsheet to track the many different assets that might go into an episode, such as animations, graphics, voice-over scripts, and storyboards. Sometimes it's helpful to toggle to these

details in a meeting, just to be able to show how much stuff is being managed for an experience.

◆ **Collaboration tools.** We love apps like Slack and Basecamp, where a team of people can chat real time, manage revisions, and start threaded discussions. This type of view can also be useful to show to stakeholders who might not otherwise realize just how much back-and-forth happens during a build process.

◆ **Videos, photos, and "day in the life" stories.** We've been known to make short videos of our team working on stuff (like this book!) and post it for people to see. Or to crowdsource a concept. This helps keep everyone engaged and interested in progress, and demystifies the process.

◆ **Lots of PowerPoint.** Yes, we use PowerPoint, like the 99.9999% of the rest of the corporate world. While Edward Tufte[3] may have had a few things to say about it (and he has some great points), we believe it can be used effectively to present information – it just takes a bit more thoughtful rendering than simply showing bullets on a slide.

Validating Content. That word "content" tends to mean different things to different people. When we say "content," we mean subject matter, topics, and information – not how it looks or how it's rendered. Separating these two aspects can be very helpful when getting validation about the accuracy and relevancy of content, because you can say, "Don't worry about how this looks. Is this what someone needs to know or do?" You can also ask about logic, flow, and message. Does it come off in the right way and is the point clearly made? Your SMEs and stakeholders can help with messaging and validate the language they use and that the audience understands.

Setting Expectations. Ed Catmull, the president of Pixar Animation Studios, writes in his book *Creativity, Inc.* about the concept of every Pixar film starting out as an "ugly baby."[4] The same will be true of many of the experiences you will create. Make sure to set the expectation that the first part of the process is messy. That the outputs are really no more than "containers for complexity." And that, as design begins, the contributed content and initial storyboards will not be pretty in the first few iterations. Once content is validated, you can begin to add polish (layout, graphics, video), and the outputs for your experience will start to come to life. You'll be amazed – and so will your stakeholders – that by the time it's GEFRN, the output often doesn't resemble what you started with. If you've done the process correctly, GEFRN is still a hundred times better than the original.

Be Thankful for Feedback – And Use What Makes Sense. Not all the feedback that you'll receive as you iterate will be helpful or useful. You can always say "Thank you" for the feedback, and then decide whether or not it makes sense to factor it in. Stay focused on the outcome, and have empathy for the humans who will experience what you create.

When Are You Done?

If progress is what matters, how do we know when to stop? When is it GEFRN? Here are some examples of progress and checkpoints that we use within the stages of the process.

- ◆ **Show the work behind what it takes to define an outcome.** Figuring out the outcome can take several working sessions, codifying in a document, validating with an Executive Sponsor ... and can take four to six weeks of work to get to agreement. Document everything along the way, then tell a story about it in pictures or screen shots.
- ◆ **Be able to talk about how many people it takes to scope an initiative.** Understanding the effort and work for an initiative takes discussion amongst the right people who all understand the outcome. Even still, many of these types of initiatives can only define so much detail up front, and getting four to six people to agree on a scope is a big effort in and of itself!
- ◆ **Establish approval checkpoints at each stage of the process.** For example, when the sponsor approves the architected experience as a whole, you can then move to Design.

♦ **Establish approval checkpoints for content.** When the SME engages, provides feedback, and approves the accuracy of the content, you can then focus on storyboards and designing the interactions and episodes.

♦ **Use internal validation checkpoints.** When a Designer validates that an output has been built according to the design. You have iterated a few times with others' input being incorporated.

♦ **Ongoing communication and posting of revisions.** The Designer communicates with the Experience Manager during the iterations, posting each version with specific notes about additional information needed in the storyboard. This allows the Experience Manager and other stakeholders to see the design process in action and provide feedback as it progresses.

♦ **Daily sync calls.** Teams host short, daily syncs whose purpose is to give reports on work, to show progress, and to call out any obstacles. This allows other team members to see work in action on a day-to-day basis, and also to step in to help each other overcome challenges.

♦ **Team callouts.** Any team member, at any point, can show progress by calling out obstacles. Team members and leaders can take the view that, the sooner they know about a problem, the faster they can figure out how to solve it and how much time it'll take.

Keep in mind that your stakeholders are under pressure to deliver results, and this can cause anxiety when they can't get visibility into what's being done – particularly if you are trying to do the upfront work of Envision, Environment, and Architect that so many organizations tend to skip. As the title of this chapter states, if you want to diffuse that anxiety, show progress, however you can. It's all that matters in the journey to Radical Outcomes.

ACTIVATE

13

Activate Radical Outcomes

We've had three big ideas at Amazon that we've stuck with for 18 years and they're the reason we're successful: Put the customer first. Invent. And be patient.

—Jeff Bezos, founder of Amazon

"Heads up, Olivia." The stage manager stuck his head around the door to the green room. "10 minutes. Need anything?"

"All set, thanks," replied Olivia, taking a swig of water from the bottle on the table. She checked herself in the mirror for what seemed to be the hundredth time, then walked the perimeter of the room, which had several couches at one end, and dressing tables with lighted mirrors on the other. One of the couches had an end table on each side, and Olivia stopped at one of the end tables to look at a printed booklet that had been left behind, perhaps by a speaker who'd occupied this same room the night before. Or a musician? She picked up the booklet, thumbed through it, and smiled. The cover of the booklet showed a group of musicians floating in what appeared to be a zero-gravity chamber. She'd heard of this group – more like performance art, the musicians would produce crazy videos that seemed impossible to make. "Cool," she murmured, thinking what a great example it would be to reference in her speech.

She crossed back to the dressing table side of the room and looked at a collection of papers – slide printouts, with slick photographs and brief, elegant-looking text – all stuck to the wall in a sequence. *Okay, let's just go through the flow once more before showtime*, she thought.

They gave us an impossible task, but it only seemed impossible because of the way we were used to working. Check.

We shifted our process and our mindset. Check.

Here are some of the things that we did along the way. In three months, we launched an experience for 300 sellers. There was a huge push at the end, getting it out, up, communicated, ensuring people knew it was available, that managers were prepared. But that wasn't the end of it . . . Olivia placed her index finger on one of the slides. *It was really just the beginning.*

Olivia spoke the talking points out loud to herself as she pointed to each slide on the wall.

"Just like we described over and over to the stakeholders, we created the experience so that it could be serviced and measured through time, making ongoing tweaks and updates to ensure that the outcomes continue to be met." She took another swig of water.

"But first I'm sure you want to know about the results. Well, we had to wait a bit for those to come in. Actually, it wasn't so much waiting, really, it was more like we were watching people go through it, tracking the metrics, seeing if and when people stalled out."

"Don't forget to add in the part about how the data and analytics team was surprised by those requests you made." Nimit's voice came from the open door. Olivia hadn't heard him. "Sorry, Olivia – the door was open a little bit and I heard you talking to yourself," he said, smiling. "Nothing new there."

"That's cool, Nimit. Right. Thanks for the reminder." Her voice went back to presentation mode. "When we asked the analytics team to track stuff for us, they said they'd never seen these types of requests from our group before. 'Measuring the audience's time to quota? We thought you guys were only interested in how many people attended,' that's what they would say to us." She looked at Nimit. "I was going to say that over here," and pointed to a slide further down the stack.

"That's fine, all good, I don't want to mess with your presentation just before you go onstage. I'm sure it's in there," said Nimit.

He looked at the printouts on the wall. "You always did like to go analog for these types of things, Olivia. Anyway, I came by to just say congratulations again. Who would have thought 18 months ago, you'd be doing a speech like this, telling your story?"

"It's not just my story, Nimit. There was a whole –"

"Team. Yes, of course. It's remarkable, that kind of productivity. But the numbers. That's why Rivers is singling you out for this event. He wants to show how much it moved the needle. I saw him in the audience, by the way. Maya is there too. I think, once you wowed her in that session where you brought her into the war room to show the progress – you got a fan for life!"

Olivia waved at Nimit, as if waving away a distraction, and looked at one slide on the wall, the one that she and team had called "The Money Slide" when they were creating the presentation. She spoke for emphasis:

"Nine months after launch, new-hire sellers who went through the experience hit 139% of quota in four months. Those who didn't hit 80% quota in that same time frame. Which was essentially where things were when we started on this," said Olivia.

"You gotta let that sink in, Olivia. 139% of quota in their first four months? Multiply that times, how many sellers now have gone through, and they're staying in role since they started?" said Nimit. "Two thousand?"

"And growing," said Olivia.

"And it's being maintained by two people?" He shook his head. "Amazing."

There was a knock on the door. "Five minutes, Olivia," said the stage manager.

"It basically never stops. We never stop making sure that it stays connected to the outcome. But, man – it's so easy now to update," said Olivia.

"Well, and it helps that you are now on these councils where you are sought out as the person who knows how to deliver, and they're involving you earlier on," said Nimit.

Olivia looked at the last slide – a photo of the team who created the experience, posing in the war room, the walls messy with print-outs and the table scattered with laptops and papers. She placed her finger on the slide. The extraordinary team.

"Thousands of outputs, none of them wasted. Pretty radical," said Nimit.

Olivia straightened up and opened the door. "Show's on," she said. It was clear to her how she wanted to end this speech.

Keep the Momentum

We've covered a lot in this book. Each chapter has different methods and ideas you can implement to see what works for you and what doesn't. Just like the experience that Olivia and her team created, the work and adjustments never stop. We have been iterating and adjusting and learning for years – and this book is just one codified example of what we know right now!

We strongly identify with the quote from Jeff Bezos at the beginning of this chapter where he says: "Be patient."

Shifting the way in which you and your teams work, in order to produce Radical Outcomes, doesn't just happen overnight, just like people don't learn overnight. We try to focus on how to make small shifts on a constant basis. We ask ourselves, what would it look like if we did something 5% differently? And then again, 5% more? Over time, the changes add up.

We believe that those positive differences, even if small, can make a massive change in the results for your team and the company you work for. We all know that, unfortunately, there is no silver bullet to making big changes. There is, however, hard work, dedication, and progress – and doing so collaboratively is the biggest accelerator that we have been able to find. If you think about making small shifts in the way you work with your team and with stakeholders, it can lessen the intensity that you may feel in having to drive a massive change result. Focus on creating an environment in which you can make steady impact that will show consistent results. Then, the moment will arrive when, a few years down the road, you'll be able to look back and say, "Wow – we have made such massive strides." It's only with hindsight that you'll be able to see how radical a shift you can make.

Indespensible Wisdom

One of our favorite books, Ed Catmull's *Creativity, Inc.*, has some wonderful words of wisdom that we consider indispensable.

◆ Failure isn't a necessary evil. In fact, it isn't evil at all. It is a necessary consequence of doing something new.

◆ Excellent, quality, and good should be earned words. Attributed by others to us, not proclaimed by us about ourselves.

◆ Trust doesn't mean that you trust someone won't screw up – it means you trust them even when they do screw up.

◆ The healthiest organizations are made up of departments whose agendas differ, but whose goals are interdependent. If one agenda wins, we all lose.[1]

The best advice we can give:

◆ Stay curious.
◆ Focus on outcomes and the audience, use the process, and the rest will follow.
◆ Ensemble your heart out.
◆ Say "I don't know."
◆ Not having the answer is . . . human.
◆ Be a back-haver.
◆ See your work as a part of driving radical outcomes for your teams and success for your customers, not as an extension of yourself.
◆ Let go of making your work perfect on your own – if your team is dedicated to succeeding together, you can iterate all the way to GEFRN and beyond!
◆ Overcommunicate, especially when you are struggling; you can show progress just by telling your team the challenge you're facing, and they probably have suggestions to help you.
◆ Get comfortable with change; expect it.

Radical Outcomes are absolutely within reach for you and your teams. Go ahead and activate them!

Notes

Chapter 1: The Why

1. Jeff Bezos, "2017 Letter to Shareholders," published April 18, 2018, from Amazon.com, Inc.'s investor relations website, http://phx.corporate-ir.net/phoenix.zhtml?c=97664&p=irol-reportsannual.

2. "About Us," Sales Enablement Society, 2018, https://sesociety.connectedcommunity.org/about-us/about-us-. One example of the momentum of the "enablement profession" is The Sales Enablement Society, which grew from 50 members to over 2,500 in the span of 18 months and hosts conferences, online communities, and a mission to elevate the profession of Sales Enablement.

3. Scott Santucci (chief growth catalyst, Growth Enablement Ecosystems), interview by Katherine Shao, January 2018 https://vimeo.com/251395306/a01f313da3.

4. "Meet the Modern Learner: Engaging the Overwhelmed, Distracted, and Impatient Employee," Infographic, Bersin by Deloitte, Deloitte Consulting LLP, 2014, https://login.bersin.com/Login.aspx?p=http://bersinone.bersin.com/resources/research/?docid=18066&h=1; Daniel Kahneman, *Thinking, Fast and Slow* (New York: Farrar, Straus and Giroux, 2011). Kahneman's book provides a solid basis of studies for the view of information overload; Daniel Pink, *When: The Scientific Secrets of Perfect Timing* (New York: Riverhead Books, 2018). Daniel Pink carries the idea further in his recent publication.

5. Kenneth P. Pitts (PhD, cognitive neuroscientist), interview by Katherine Shao, April 3, 2018.

6. Josh Bersin, "The Disruption of Digital Learning: Ten Things We Have Learned," *Josh Bersin (Insights on Corporate Talent, Learning, Leadership, and HR Technology)*, March 27, 2017, https://joshbersin.com/2017/03/the-disruption-of-digital-learning-ten-things-we-have-learned/.

Chapter 2: The Process: Don't Leave Home without It

1. Hal Crook, *Ready, Aim, Improvise!: Exploring the Basics of Jazz Improvisation* (Alfred Music, 1999), 271–272.

2. Josh Bersin, Deloitte Consulting LLP, "A New Paradigm For Corporate Training: Learning in the Flow of Work," June 3, 2018, https://joshbersin .com/2018/06/a-new-paradigm-for-corporate-training-learning-in-the-flow-of-work/#_ftn1.

3. "Agile Manifesto," 2001, https://www.agilealliance.org/wp-content/ uploads/2017/10/Agile-Manifesto-Black-and-White.pdf?utm_ source=edit-profile-page-manifesto-link&utm_medium=manifesto-download-link.

Chapter 3: Create Your Ensemble

1. Charles Duhigg, *Smarter Faster Better: The Transformative Power of Real Productivity* (New York: Random House, 2016), 38–42, 46, 50–51, 68.

2. RACI Model, from *A Guide to the Project Management Body of Knowledge (PMBOK® Guide),* fifth ed. (Newtown Square, PA: Project Management Institute, 2013), 262.

3. According to Edmondson, "Psychological safety is a belief that one will not be punished or humiliated for speaking up with ideas, questions, concerns, or mistakes." From "What Is Psychological Safety and Why Is It the Key to Great Teamwork?," Impraise Blog, https://blog.impraise.com/ 360-feedback/what-is-psychological-safety-and-why-is-it-the-key-to-great-teamwork-performance-review. Originally from Edmondson's dissertation.

Chapter 4: Let Go of What You Know

1. Destin Sandlin, "The Backwards Brain Bicycle – Smarter Every Day," published on YouTube April 24, 2015, video, https://youtu.be/ MFzDaBzBlL0.

2. Daniel Kahneman, *Thinking, Fast and Slow* (New York: Farrar, Straus and Giroux, 2011).

3. It's our hunch that this tectonic shift for the workplace will happen relatively sooner for knowledge workers, the tech sector, B2B and B2C businesses; and will happen relatively later for academia, government, and other heavily subsidized entities that tend to change later than most sectors.

Chapter 5: It's Business Outcome Time

1. Claudine Beaumont "Bill Gates's Dream: A Computer in Every Home," *The Telegraph*, June 2008, https://www.telegraph.co.uk/technology/3357701/Bill-Gatess-dream-A-computer-in-every-home.html.

2. Ibid.

3. Scott Santucci (chief growth catalyst, Growth Enablement Ecosystems), interview by Katherine Shao, January 2018 https://vimeo.com/251395306/a01f313da3.

4. When it comes to the things people need to know and do in the workplace, there are some investments that are viewed as nonnegotiable, such as compliance. Every business needs to be compliant, and its importance cannot be overlooked.

5. "Working in a New Way: Modeling the Human Side of Organizational Success," *Human Capital Institute and Oxygen,* February 15, 2018, http://www.hci.org/hr-research/working-new-way-modeling-human-side-organizational-success?utm_source=HCIwebsite&utm_medium=PDF&utm_campaign=new-ways-research-paper.

6. James Harter, Frank Schmidt, and Corey Keyes, "Well-Being in the Workplace and Its Relationship to Business Outcomes: A Review of the Gallup Studies," in *Flourishing: The Positive Person and the Good Life*, ed. Corey Keyes and Jonathan Haidt (Washington, DC: American Psychological Association, 2003), 205–224, http://media.gallup.com/documents/whitePaper—Well-BeingInTheWorkplace.pdf.

7. Annette Franz, "What Are Your Business Outcomes?" July 12, 2016, *CX Journey*, https://www.cx-journey.com/2016/07/what-are-your-business-outcomes.html.

Chapter 6: Putting Divisions Out of Business

1. "The Rise of the Social Enterprise (2018 Global Human Capital Trends)," Deloitte Insights, https://www2.deloitte.com/content/dam/insights/us/articles/HCTrends2018/2018-HCtrends_Rise-of-the-social-enterprise.pdf.

Chapter 7: The Experience Is Human

1. Josh Bersin, "The Disruption of Digital Learning: Ten Things We Have Learned," March 27, 2017, *Josh Bersin (Insights on Corporate Talent, Learning, Leadership, and HR Technology,* https://joshbersin.com/2017/03/the-disruption-of-digital-learning-ten-things-we-have-learned/.

2. "2017 Workplace Learning Report: How Modern L&D Pros Are Tackling Top Challenges," February 7, 2017, *LinkedIn Learning*, https://learning .linkedin.com/blog/learning-thought-leadership/introducing-the-2017-workplace-learning-report—top-trends—cha.

3. "Working in a New Way: Modeling the Human Side of Organizational Success," 2018, Oxygen, 19, https://oxygenexp.com/wp-content/uploads/2018/06/Working%20in%20a%20New%20Way_Web.pdf.

Chapter 8: Why We Can't Live without Architecture

1. Kevin J. Singh, "21 Rules for a Successful Life in Architecture," EntreArchitect.com, August 24, 2014, https://entrearchitect.com/2014/08/24/21-rules-for-a-successful-life-in-architecture/.

2. Kenneth P. Pitts (PhD, cognitive neuroscientist), interview by Katherine Shao, April 3, 2018.

3. Daniel Kahneman, *Thinking, Fast and Slow* (New York: Farrar, Straus and Giroux, 2011).

4. Daniel Pink, *When: The Scientific Secrets of Perfect Timing* (New York: Riverhead Books, 2018).

Chapter 10: Not Your Average Design

1. Edward Tufte, *The Cognitive Style of PowerPoint: Pitching Out Corrupts Within*, second edition (Cheshire, CT: Graphics Press, 2006).

2. Daniel Kahneman, *Thinking, Fast and Slow* (New York: Farrar, Straus and Giroux, 2013), 60.

3. Ibid.

4. Ibid.

Chapter 11: Knowing What Is Good Enough

1. Ed Catmull, *Creativity, Inc.: Overcoming the Unseen Forces That Stand in the Way of True Inspiration* (New York: Random House, 2014).

2. Kathryn Schulz, *Being Wrong: Adventures in the Margin of Error* (New York: Ecco, 2011), 5.

3. Ibid.

4. Jeff Bezos, "2017 Letter to Shareholders," published April 18, 2018, from the Amazon.com, Inc. investor relations website, http://phx.corporate-ir .net/phoenix.zhtml?c=97664&p=irol-reportsannual.

Chapter 12: Progress Is All That Matters

1. "Steve Jobs Special Issue," *Bloomberg Businessweek Magazine*, October 10, 2011, https://www.bloomberg.com/magazine/businessweek/11_42.

2. "9.1.2.1 Organization Charts and Position Descriptions," *A Guide to the Project Management Body of Knowledge (PMBOK® Guide)*, fifth edition (Newtown Square, PA: Project Management Institute, 2013), 261.

3. Edward Tufte, *The Cognitive Style of PowerPoint: Pitching Out Corrupts Within,* second edition (Cheshire, CT: Graphics Press, 2006).

4. Ed Catmull, Creativity, Inc.: Overcoming the Unseen Forces That Stand in the Way of True Inspiration (New York: Random House, 2014), 131–138, 141–142.

Chapter 13: Activate Radical Outcomes

1. Ed Catmull, Creativity, Inc.: Overcoming the Unseen Forces That Stand in the Way of True Inspiration (New York: Random House, 2014), 316–319.

Acknowledgments

*R*adical Outcomes was created using the process, philosophy, and mindset outlined in its pages. I was not a lone author and, without the help of people on my team, there is very little chance that we could have hit our deadlines.

I want to first and foremost thank Katherine Shao. This book would not be written without Katherine. She spent hundreds of hours with me prior to the decision to write the book exploring, debating, and clarifying the world of our work at Oxygen. After the codification and documentation of so much of the work that Oxygen does and the point of view we carry – which became a basis for this book – Katherine took on the challenge of taking the raw material and shaped the narrative logically and cohesively. Her comradery and focus on progress and iteration was unparalleled, even as we also continued our client work during the authoring process. Thank you so much for being on this journey with me – I literally could not have done it without you.

There are many others at Oxygen to thank for their roles during this journey: thank you to Jadyn Tichy for keeping us on track and making sure we hit our deadlines; to Simon Pollock for editing, reading, researching, and fleshing out chapters as we went along; to Nick Rampey for supporting us, bringing all of the materials together, tracking down all of the little things we had to document, and thinking of different avenues to promote the book; and lastly to Vladimir Mirkovic at TransArt Design for the dedication to creating our visuals in order to bring the written ideas to life.

So many other people – colleagues, clients, and confidantes – have been with me on this journey to build a business. They have helped me figure out the best way to approach and solve client work and supported me as I continued to push a point of view that wasn't just an easy answer – it was a way to make real changes and try to figure out new ways to collaborate and succeed. Thank you

185

for being on this journey with me: Jean-Philippe Mula, Diane Legg, Donna Hadaller, Natasha Zweig, Rob O'Such, Scott Santucci, John Byrum, Brett Scallan, Jeff Cleator, Teresa Loo, Jennifer Olsen, Geoff McDonald, Jim Rowe, Peter Buck, and so many amazing clients.

About the Author

Juliana Stancampiano is an entrepreneur and the CEO of Oxygen. For more than 15 years, she has worked with Fortune 500 companies, both in them and for them. This experience, along with the research that Oxygen conducts and the articles she has published, helped to shape the perspective that Oxygen embraces and that you have read about in this book.

Index

Page references followed by *fig* indicate an illustrated figure.